THIRTY DAYS

OF
Prayer

FOR FOSTER PARENTS &
ADOPTIVE FAMILIES

CRYSTAL DENISE HARRISON

Thirty Days of Prayer for Foster Parents & Adoptive Families

Copyright © 2025 by Crystal D. Harrison M.Ed.,

Published by Grace 4 Purpose, Publishing Co. LLC

ISBN: 979-8-9926893-3-4

Editing by: Grace 4 Purpose, Publishing Co. LLC

Book cover design by Grace 4 Purpose, Publishing Co. LLC

Printed and bound in the United States of America

Thirty Days of Prayer for Foster Parents

&

Adoptive Families

By: Crystal Denise Harrison, M.Ed.

Dedication

In Honor of Mekhi James Harrison and Micah Timothy
Harrison

Both of you were mighty men of valor and honor in the
making, who touched our lives in ways that are
immeasurable. You have left an imprint on your father's
heart and mine for so many reasons; causing me to
smirk and smile as I am reminded of you both and some
of your unforgettable antics.

The football photo of the two of you standing on the
front porch is forever etched in my heart, and the story
behind it still brings laughter to my soul. Though two
separate individuals, you were, in so many ways, one
and the same you were "The Twinz!"

Your energy, sarcasm, dry humor, laughter, moments of
pure pettiness, and your unwavering love for one
another and for our family will forever be missed. The
Harrison Twinz that is who you were and who you will
always be remembered as.

H.O.E ~ Harrison Over Everything!

Mekhi, what was initially my annoyance at you carving those letters into our living room wall has now become a masterpiece in my eyes.

You are two beloved souls who embraced our family through the miracle of foster care and adoption. This journal stands as a testament to the power of prayer, love, faith, and the unwavering belief in God's plan for each of our lives. It reflects the impact we can have on a generation of God's gifts. Children who have been misplaced in our society and thrust into hardship early in life for reasons beyond their control.

As foster and adoptive families, we each have the sacred opportunity to alter the lives of these "gifts of God" forever through the grace of God operating within us unconditionally. My prayer is that this journal encourages other families to seek the very heartbeat of God as they care for the children He has, or will, entrust into their hearts.

Through the pages of this journal, we share our journey of prayer, reflection, and gratitude for the lives that God entrusted to my husband Jay, and me. May it also become a space where you can pour out your heart to God offering prayers of thanksgiving for the gift of family, and petitions for His continued guidance, and blessings over your children just as we have done for Mekhi and Micah, and so many other children that God has placed within our home and hearts.

As we have documented our prayers and experiences together, may this journal serve as a reminder of the incredible journey we have traveled as a family through fostering and adoption for more than thirty-five years. May it be a source of strength in challenging times and a beacon of hope as you witness God's faithfulness and love in every area of your life.

I pray that you use this prayer journal with open hearts and minds ready to deepen your relationship with God and nurture spiritual growth for yourself, your family, and the precious gifts God has entrusted to you, just as we have for our sons, Mekhi and Micah (The Twinz). May the prayers within these pages unite your family in love and strengthen your bond, reminding you that God's love surrounds you always in every circumstance you may face.

In faith and gratitude,
Love Mom

Thank You:

Jay Jr., Juanita, Jessika, Katyce, Robert, and Romesha (Brittany our bonus daughter); dad and I thank you with hearts overflowing with gratitude for the incredible blessing that each of you have been in our lives. Thank you for your openness, generosity, and willingness to embrace foster children as a part of our family.

Lord, we thank You for the love that our children have shown, as they have welcomed foster children into our home with open arms and open hearts. Their capacity to share their space, their time, and their parents reflects Your selfless love and compassion in and through them.

Father, we are grateful for their acceptance and understanding during times of change and adjustment that have occurred multiple times within our family. Thank You for giving them hearts that are willing to share and support other children; knowing that every child deserves a loving and nurturing environment that will ultimately guide them to You.

We praise You for the kindness that they have demonstrated daily, as they built friendships, offered comfort, redirection, and created a sense of belonging for foster children who were experiencing an unsurmountable amount of uncertainty in their lives.

Acts of kindness that have reflected Your unconditional love and grace to the Twinz, each other, and dad and I will not go unnoticed especially by the Father.

Father, I pray that You would bless our children with Your strength and resilience as they navigate the joys and challenges of tragically losing both of their twin brothers; Mekhi and Micah. May they continue to grow in empathy, patience, and a deeper understanding of Your love for all of Your children seeking a home with unconditional love, support guidance and friendship.

Father, grant us the continued wisdom and guidance as we seek to nurture and support our children along their journey. Help us to continue to create a home filled with love, acceptance, and unity, where each of our children feel valued and cherished regardless of what life has challenged them with.

Thank You, Father, for the privilege and responsibility of parenting Your gifts. May Your light shine through our family, bringing hope and healing to every life that we come in contact with and beyond.

Love Mommy

Foreword

By Overseer Jay Timothy Harrison, Sr.

We welcome you to join us on our journey of prayer and reflection as an adoptive family. Within these pages, you hold not just a journal, but a sacred gateway to deep communion with our Father in Heaven.

As the founder of the Keys for Change Prophetic Intercessory Prayer Network, my primary responsibility and calling is to cultivate an atmosphere of intercession that honors the Father. Through this work, we develop Intercessory Prayer Leaders (IPLs) who are equipped to teach the biblical principles surrounding the purpose of prayer, the posture of prayer, and the power of prayer.

Within the Father's intercessory community, I have personally witnessed the transformative power of prayer and how it can heal hearts, renew faith, and bring direction to the lives of both believers and non-believers alike.

This Prayer Journal for Foster Parents & Adoptive Families is more than a collection of scriptures, prayers, and reflection pages. It is an invitation a sacred call to enter into conversation with the Father on behalf of the precious gifts He has entrusted to our care and to yours.

Each entry offers an opportunity to pour out your heart, to seek guidance, to express gratitude, and to find comfort in the presence of the Almighty.

Over the years, I have come to understand that prayer is far more than a religious practice it is a divine dialogue that shapes our souls, strengthens our faith, and aligns our will with the Father's purpose for our lives. My hope is that, as you embark on your journey as a resource parent, these pages will become a sacred repository of your time with the Father—moments of vulnerability and resilience, of joy and revelation.

May this journal become a trusted companion on your spiritual path, guiding you closer to the heart of the Father with each prayer you pray. May it stand as a testament to His faithfulness to the way He answers prayers, transforms lives, and reveals His love through every circumstance.

I pray that you are inspired to deepen your relationship with the One who hears every prayer, holds every tear, and directs every heart with genuine love and concern for His children His gifts.

In the Matchless Name of Jesus,
Overseer Jay Timothy Harrison, Sr.
Keys for Change Prophetic Intercessory Prayer Network

Day One ~ God's Divine Plan

Scripture

> *"For I know the plans I have for you,"*
> *declares the Lord,*
> *"plans to prosper you and not to harm you,*
> *plans to give you a future and a hope."*
> *Jeremiah 29:11 (KJV)*

Prayer

Father,
We come before You with grateful hearts, thanking You for the precious gifts of Mekhi and Micah. These two little boys, whom You so graciously placed in our lives, have filled our hearts with love, joy, and divine purpose. We praise You for the beauty of Your plan that brought us together, and we trust that Your hand has been guiding every step of this journey.

Lord, we pray that their hearts will come to know Your love and grace as deeply as we have. May they grow in wisdom, strength, and kindness, knowing that they are fearfully and wonderfully made in Your image. Surround them with Your protection and favor as they navigate life, and may they always find comfort and confidence in Your presence.

We lift up their future before You, Father. May their paths be filled with opportunities, blessings, and hope. Help us as parents to nurture them with patience, compassion, and understanding. Teach us to raise them in Your truth so that they may become the mighty men of valor You created them to be.

In Jesus' Name, Amen.

Reflection: Meet the Twins

It was 2008, and I had just relocated to Chester, Pennsylvania, and beginning a new job in Philadelphia. It was there that I met two remarkable little boys named Mekhi and Micah.

One of my first encounters with Micah happened during my very first week on the job. I was called to assist during one of his more challenging moments a full-blown meltdown. The scene was intense and chaotic, yet in the midst of it, something beautiful happened. Micah and I connected. I can't explain it fully, but I knew, even then that a bond had been formed in that moment one that time, distance, and circumstance would never erase.

Despite that unforgettable introduction, there was something magnetic about the twins something radiant. Both were bursting with energy, personality, and a joy for life that was contagious. They were like two little batteries, fully charged, lighting up every room they entered. Their boundless enthusiasm, quick humor, and curiosity made every day an adventure.

Mekhi and Micah weren't just twins they were a force of nature. From the very beginning, I knew they would hold a special place in my heart forever.

Reflection of the Day

_____

_____

_____

_____

_____

_____

_____

_____

_____

_____

_____

_____

_____

Day Two ~ A Father to the Fatherless

Scripture

> *"A father to the fatherless, a defender of*
> *widows, is God in His holy dwelling."*
> *Psalm 68:5 (KJV)*

Prayer

Father,
We come before You with grateful hearts, thanking
You for the way You orchestrate every detail of our
lives with perfect timing and divine purpose. Even on
that special day when Jay first met Mekhi and Micah we
felt Your presence guiding each moment. We know that
nothing You do is by accident, but part of the beautiful
plan You have written for our family.

Lord, we saw Your hand at work as You began forming
a bond that only You could create. Mekhi, and Micah
who longed for a father, found in Jay a man who would
love, protect, and guide them with grace and strength.
Thank You for calling Jay to this sacred role and
preparing his heart long before that day arrived. Thank
You for making this divine connection so evident and so
filled with Your peace.

Father, we ask that You continue to bless the relationship between Jay, Mekhi, and Micah. May their bond grow stronger with each passing day rooted in love, understanding, and mutual respect. Help Jay to be the loving father You have called him to be, and let Mekhi, and Micah continually experience Your love through his words, actions, and presence.

We thank You for the gift of these two boys; for their laughter, their joy, and their remarkable spirit. We rest in the truth of Psalm 68:5, that You are indeed "a Father to the fatherless." Thank You for fulfilling that promise through Jay, and for the healing You continue to bring to our family.

May their journey together be one of restoration, growth, and unwavering love. We place our family in Your hands, trusting You as the firm foundation upon which it is built. Grant us wisdom and guidance as we walk this path together. Protect our hearts, unite us in faith, and let Your love be the thread that binds us as one.

In Jesus' Name, Amen.

Reflection: The Twins Needed a Father

I remember the day as clearly as if it were yesterday. When Ms. Sheila came to the school to drop off the twins, she paused for a moment before asking a question that would change our lives forever.

"Would you and your husband consider adopting Mekhi and Micah?"

Her words struck my heart with instant clarity. I knew deep within that it was God's will for me to say yes, but I also knew I needed to speak with my husband before making such a life-changing decision. So, I paused, closed my eyes, and prayed for direction.

In that quiet moment, I felt God speak to my heart: "The boys need a father."

It was as if His words were whispered directly to my spirit, giving me the confirmation I needed. This wasn't just an opportunity it was a divine assignment.

With a heart full of peace, I shared with Jay what God had placed on my heart and invited him to visit the Head Start program where I worked. I knew that God had already prepared his heart for what was to come.

When Jay arrived at the school and met Mekhi and Micah, it was as if the boys already knew. Their eyes lit up with excitement, and they eagerly surrounded him, as though they had been waiting for this moment all along. In that instant, it was undeniable God had orchestrated this meeting. Jay wasn't just visiting that day; he was stepping into his calling as their father.

Scripture tells us,

> *"He predestined us for adoption to sonship through Jesus Christ, in accordance with His pleasure and will." Ephesians 1:5 (KJV)*

That verse came alive in my spirit that day. We witnessed firsthand how God's plan unfolds with grace, precision, and purpose.

That moment marked the beginning of a new chapter one filled with faith, love, and an unbreakable bond that would forever connect our family with these two extraordinary boys. God's hand had written this story long before we could see it, and we stepped forward in faith, trusting Him completely with what He had begun.

Reflection of the Day

_____

_____

_____

_____

_____

_____

_____

_____

_____

_____

_____

_____

_____

Day Three ~ Stuck Like Glue

Scripture

> *"So do not fear, for I am with you;*
> *do not be dismayed, for I am your God.*
> *I will strengthen you and help you;*
> *I will uphold you with my righteous right*
> *hand." Isaiah 41:10 (KJV)*

Prayer

Heavenly Father,

We come before You with hearts full of gratitude and love as we reflect on our time with Mekhi and Micah. Thank You, Lord, for blessing us with these two amazing boys and for the joy of creating memories together as a family.

As we remember our first family vacation, we also recall the fear and uncertainty that filled Mekhi and Micah's hearts. They thought we might be sending them away to another home. But You, Lord, were already at work healing wounds, calming fears, and revealing the strength of love.

We lift them up to You today, asking that Your peace and assurance continue to fill their hearts. Let them always feel secure in our love and commitment to them. May they know without a shadow of a doubt that they are not only loved but deeply cherished, and that they will always have a place in our hearts and in our home.

Thank You for the moment when Jay spoke words of truth and life over them. May his words, "We are stuck like glue," echo in their spirits forever, reminding them that we are a family bound together by Your unbreakable love.

Lord, help us to continually create an environment where they feel safe, valued, and deeply loved no matter where we go or what challenges we may face. We hold to Your promise in *Isaiah 41:10,* that You are our strength and our help. Father, help Mekhi and Micah to feel Your presence always to know that they are never alone and that You are their constant source of strength, security, and protection.

As we continue this journey as a family, guide us in nurturing their hearts, building trust, and showing them the depth of Your love. May every adventure, every moment, and every day remind them of Your faithfulness and of the unbreakable bond we share through You.

We thank You for the privilege of being their parents and for trusting us with such precious gifts. Teach us to lead them with wisdom, patience, and grace, knowing that You are guiding us every step of the way.

In Jesus' Name, Amen.

Reflection: Vacation Time

Our first family vacation with Mekhi and Micah was filled with excitement and anticipation. Everyone was eager as we packed our bags for the Caribbean Indoor Water Park in Lancaster, Pennsylvania a trip we knew would create unforgettable memories. We explained to the boys that this vacation was a special gift from Ms. Norma, and that they could thank her when we returned by sharing all the fun they had.

But as the packing continued, something unexpected happened. Mekhi and Micah suddenly became upset. They grabbed their new matching suitcases and began throwing clothes all over their room in frustration. Concerned, we stepped in to calm them. That's when we discovered the reason for their distress Micah believed we were sending them away to another home.

My heart sank. The fear in his eyes spoke volumes, revealing the deep scars left by instability and uncertainty.

Then Jay knelt down and spoke to them with tenderness and strength. He said, "We love you two midgets, so we are stuck like glue." His words were filled with love and reassurance. "Just trust me," he added gently. "We're going on an amazing adventure."

Mekhi, still hesitant but softening, looked up and asked quietly, "You're keeping us?"

Jay smiled and said, "Of course no matter what."

That moment changed everything. The boys needed to hear that truth that they were loved, wanted, and home for good. Jay's words became a turning point, sealing something eternal in their hearts and ours.

What began as a moment of fear became a memory of deep healing. From that day forward, our family bond grew stronger. Mekhi and Micah weren't just part of our family in name they were truly home.

That day reminded us that love is more than a feeling; it's a commitment. Through laughter, tears, and every season that followed, we lived those words "stuck like glue," and bound by love, faith, and the unwavering grace of God.

Reflection of the Day

_____

_____

_____

_____

_____

_____

_____

_____

_____

_____

_____

_____

_____

_____

Day Four ~ An Everlasting Love

Scripture

> *"I have loved you with an everlasting love;*
> *I have drawn you with unfailing*
> *kindness." Jeremiah 31:3 (KJV)*

Prayer

Heavenly Father,

We come before You today with hearts overflowing with gratitude for the gift of Micah our sweet and precious son. Thank You for the joy and innocence he brings into our lives each day. We praise You for the love You have for him a love that is pure, unshakable, and everlasting.

Lord, we lift Micah to You as he begins to experience his first emotions of affection and love, even at such a young age. Thank You for the tender heart You have given him and for the gentle ways he is learning to express love like his sweet friendship with Janiyah. Love is a beautiful gift, and even now, You are teaching him what it means.

Father, we ask for Your wisdom and guidance as Micah grows in understanding. As Jay shares fatherly counsel, may Micah learn that love is not just a feeling, but a connection that deepens with maturity, patience, and faith. Help him to know that at this age, his focus should be on learning, playing, and growing in his relationship with You and that, in Your perfect timing, You will reveal the true meaning of love.

Lord, we pray for Jay as he walks this journey beside Micah. May his words be filled with grace, warmth, and wisdom. Let his example reflect Your heart a father guiding his son to know love that honors You first. Grant him tenderness and discernment as he teaches Micah to love with kindness, respect, and understanding.

We are reminded of Your Word in *1 John 4:19 "We love because He first loved us."*

Lord, help Micah to understand that all love flows from You that Your love for him is unconditional and eternal. May he learn to love others as You love him, and to recognize that true love begins in the heart that seeks You.

Father, we place Micah in Your hands, trusting that You will lead and guide him as he continues to grow in wisdom, maturity, and grace. Surround him always with Your protection and peace. May he come to know Your heart more deeply with every passing day.

In Jesus' Name, Amen.

Reflection: I Love You

The first time Micah said, "I love you, Mom," is a moment I will never forget especially after the whirlwind of emotions that had filled our day.

It was January 5, 2009, and we had just left the courthouse. The adoption papers were signed, the case was closed, and though there was still a long journey ahead, the air felt different lighter, full of hope.

The drive home was quiet, but it was a peaceful quiet. Micah, usually full of curiosity and chatter, sat beside me in the back seat, calm and thoughtful. He reached for my hand his tiny fingers curling around mine and looked up at me with those wide, trusting eyes. After all they had endured, that simple gesture spoke volumes. It was as if he knew how much I needed that touch a wordless confirmation that he knew he was home.

When we arrived, we settled back into our routine. I was in the kitchen preparing lunch when I heard a soft voice from the living room say, "I love you, Mom."

I froze, almost uncertain I'd heard correctly. It wasn't loud or dramatic just quiet and sincere. I turned, and there he was sitting on the couch, red monster truck in hand, smiling with the kind of pure joy only a child can express. That small moment carried a power I can still feel to this day.

Tears filled my eyes as I walked over to him. My voice almost cracked with emotion as I said, "I love you too, Micah."

It wasn't just what he said it was what it meant. After all the uncertainty, all the changes, all the questions of belonging, those three words were his way of saying, "I'm home."

That moment marked something sacred. It wasn't just a child's declaration of love; it was the sealing of a promise, of healing, of trust, and of family. In that instant, every hardship, every tear, every prayer was worth it.

That first "I love you" will forever echo in my heart as a reminder of God's faithfulness His everlasting love, reflected through the heart of a little boy who finally knew he was loved beyond measure.

Reflection of the Day

_____

_____

_____

_____

_____

_____

_____

_____

_____

_____

_____

_____

_____

_____

_____

Day Five ~ Brothers for Life

Scripture

> *"How good and pleasant it is when God's people live together in unity." Psalm 133:1 (KJV)*

Prayer

Father,

We come before You with hearts full of gratitude, thanking You for the unbreakable bond You have woven between Mekhi, Micah, and Jeremiah. Lord, we recognize that You are the Creator of all relationships, and we praise You for the gift of family that goes beyond bloodlines one defined by love, loyalty, and unwavering support.

These three brothers, knit together by Your love, are a living testimony of the strength and beauty of true brotherhood.

Lord, we ask that You continue to protect and nurture this special bond between them. May their love for one another grow stronger with each passing day. Help them to look out for one another with the same devotion and compassion that You show to us. In times of joy and in times of struggle, remind them that they are brothers, united by Your everlasting love, and that nothing in this world can break the ties they share.

We are reminded of

> *"Two are better than one, because they*
> *have a good return for their labor.*
> *If either of them falls down, one can help*
> *the other up.*
> *But pity anyone who falls and has no one*
> *to help them up." Ecclesiastes 4:9–10*

Father, may Mekhi, Micah, and Jeremiah always lift each other up in love and strength. Let them be sources of encouragement and steadfast support, ready to carry one another through life's challenges and celebrate one another's victories.

We pray that their hearts remain united in spirit, just as You designed them to be. May they experience the joy of walking through life together sharing laughter, building memories, and offering comfort when life feels heavy. Let their relationship be a shining example of the power of love, family, and friendship rooted in You.

Father, may their bond overflow with peace, understanding, and joy. Teach them to build each other up, forgive quickly, and celebrate each other's unique gifts. Thank You for blessing these three young men with such a sacred brotherhood.

May their connection stand as a witness to the world that true family is not just defined by DNA, but by the heart by the love we share and the ways we reflect Your divine nature in one another. Keep them close, Lord. Let their bond remain strong, unbreakable, and everlasting.

In Jesus' Name, Amen.

Reflection: Brothers Plus One The Unbreakable Bond of Mekhi, Micah, and Jeremiah

From the very first moment that Mekhi and Micah met Jeremiah, something extraordinary happened. Even though Jeremiah was technically their nephew, it didn't take long before he became a brother in every sense of the word.

The connection between them was immediate, natural, deep, and full of the kind of love that only brothers can share. Mekhi and Micah, though older, never treated Jeremiah as anything less than one of their own. From day one, they embraced him completely, and the three of them quickly became inseparable.

Their days together were filled with laughter, games, and endless adventures. No one would have guessed that Mekhi and Micah were Jeremiah's uncles, because their bond went far beyond titles it was rooted in genuine love and unity.

The summers they spent together were some of the happiest memories they created. Whether Jeremiah was visiting Pennsylvania or the family was traveling to Virginia, their reunions were full of joy and anticipation. There were endless basketball games in the driveway, splashing and swimming, and nights filled with laughter that echoed through the house. Those moments were sacred childhood memories woven into a tapestry of the Harrison brotherhood.

Mekhi, and Micah always looked out for Jeremiah. They guided him, protected him, and made sure he was always included. Whether they were teaching him how to perfect his basketball shot or encouraging him through life's lessons, their devotion never wavered.

In turn, Jeremiah grew up with two older brothers who loved him fiercely who made him feel safe, valued, and deeply loved. Their relationship became a beautiful example of what family truly means. It wasn't about biology it was about choice, commitment, and connection.

Together, they were more than just family; they were a bond of hearts brothers who shared faith, laughter, and love that transcended distance and time.

As the years passed, that bond only grew stronger. Through every season, they carried the truth that God Himself had knit their hearts together. No matter where life leads, one thing will always remain true Mekhi, Micah, and Jeremiah are brothers for life, bound forever by love, by faith, and by the unbreakable thread of God's grace.

Reflection of the Day

_____

_____

_____

_____

_____

_____

_____

_____

_____

_____

_____

_____

Day Six ~ Lessons in Love and Patience

Scripture

> **"Fathers, do not exasperate your children; instead, bring them up in the training and instruction of the Lord."**
> *Ephesians 6:4 (KJV)*

Prayer

Father,

Teach us to parent with patience, love, forgiveness, and understanding according to Your Word. Help us to discipline with compassion and to provide guidance that reflects Your heart. May our home be a place where this precious gift *(call the name of your foster or adopted child)* feels valued, safe, and nurtured in Your ways.

Father, open doors of opportunity so that the gifts You have placed within them can be cultivated and activated. Let Your identity resonate through every decision they make.

We come before You with hearts full of gratitude for the opportunity to parent these children You have entrusted to our care. Grant us divine wisdom and strength as we strive to raise them with patience, love, and grace.

Give us understanding as we navigate the unique challenges of parenting children we did not physically birth, yet love as our own. Help us to respond to every situation with a calm and gentle spirit, showing Your love in all we do.

Fill our hearts with Your unconditional love so that we may reflect it fully to Your gifts so that they may always know they are cherished, valued, and deeply loved as Your children and ours.

Father, grant us wisdom in guiding them along the path You have ordained for their lives. Help us to teach, correct, and nurture them in ways that honor You, always seeking their best interests and eternal growth.

Protect our relationships from anger or misunderstanding. Instead, help us to communicate with kindness, respect, and patience, fostering a bond built on trust and love.

Give us discernment to recognize each child's unique gifts and needs, and courage to nurture those gifts according to Your will. May our home forever reflect Your peace, grace, and presence.

In Jesus' Name, Amen.

Reflection: The Spaghetti Dinner

It started as an ordinary evening dinner was over, and Mekhi and Micah were supposed to clean up the kitchen, a task they'd done countless times before. But, as any parent of teenagers knows, the ordinary can turn extraordinary in the blink of an eye.

The twins, full of their usual energy and playful competitiveness, began arguing over whose turn it was to wash the dishes. What started as a harmless disagreement quickly spiraled into a full-blown food fight. Within seconds, cooked spaghetti was flying through the air, clinging to walls, furniture, and even the ceiling. It looked like a pasta explosion had gone off in the dining room.

I stood there part shocked, part frustrated trying to decide if I should laugh or cry. My first instinct was to raise my voice. I was disappointed, irritated, and completely bewildered. But as the words came out, I felt the Lord reminding me that my reaction wouldn't teach the lesson they needed to learn.

That's when Jay stepped in with wisdom and calm. Instead of simply fussing at them, he suggested that their consequence should fit the mess they made:

cleaning the walls and repainting the dining room. It wasn't punishment it was restoration.

And so, armed with buckets of soapy water, scrub brushes, and reluctant sighs, the twins got to work. They scrubbed spaghetti sauce off the walls and wiped down every surface. When that was done, they repainted the dining room learning that real responsibility means repairing what you've damaged.

Later that night, while having a quiet moment to reflect. I apologized for raising my voice and explained that my frustration came from love and a desire for them to do better. Mekhi, with his trademark humor, smirked and said, "Yeah, but Micah got us in trouble, so we deserved it."

Micah, exhausted from cleaning, looked at me and said, "Next time, can you just yell at us? I'm tired."

We all laughed, and in that moment, I realized the beauty hidden within the chaos. The lesson wasn't just about responsibility it was about grace, growth, and learning together.

That night, we each walked away with something valuable. The twins learned that actions have consequences, and I learned that love requires patience even in the middle of a spaghetti storm. Parenting doesn't always go perfectly, but when handled with wisdom and forgiveness, even the messiest moments can become memories that shape both hearts and homes.

Reflection of the Day

_____

_____

_____

_____

_____

_____

_____

_____

_____

_____

_____

_____

_____

_____

Day Seven ~ Gifts That Serve Others

Scripture

> *"Each of you should use whatever gift you have received to serve others,*
> *as faithful stewards of God's grace in its various forms." 1 Peter 4:10 (KJV)*

Prayer

Father,

Thank You for the unique gifts and talents You have placed within me. I pray that through Your strength, wisdom, and guidance, I will use these gifts to lead and nurture the precious children You have entrusted to my care.

Father, help me to guide this foster or adopted gift *(call the name of your child)* toward the purpose and destiny You designed for them before they were even formed in the womb. Remind me that their life is not an accident, but a divine assignment, crafted by Your hand and filled with promise.

I pray that every adult who comes into this child's life will be aligned with Your purpose as servants, and encouragers who will speak life, love, and wisdom into their journey. Surround them with mentors, teachers, and caregivers who reflect Your grace and help them walk boldly into their God-given identity.

May our child grow to recognize and use their own gifts in service to others, becoming a faithful steward of Your grace in all its forms.

In Jesus' Name, Amen.

Reflection: A Lesson in Giving in Micah and Mekhi's Lawn Service

One summer, Mekhi and Micah decided they wanted to help out around the neighborhood and make a little money for their upcoming birthday. Armed with their dad's lawn mower, a couple of rakes, grass seed, and the trusty weed-whacker, they set out on a mission. Their goal was simple to work hard, help their neighbors, and earn a few dollars along the way.

They started with the neighbors in Sun Village, and before long, word spread to the folks on Elsinore Place. They charged $20 per yard, and soon, their services were in high demand. From one lawn to the next, the twins poured their energy into every job, their laughter echoing through the streets.

But what stood out most wasn't the money they earned it was the kindness they showed. If a neighbor couldn't pay the full price, Mekhi and Micah still did the work. Sometimes they accepted a cold soda water, a small snack, or just a heartfelt "thank you" as payment. Their willingness to serve without expecting anything in return revealed hearts full of generosity and compassion.

By the end of the week, they had earned a little over $178.00. But when they sat down to talk with their dad, the lesson became about more than hard work it was about honoring God through giving. Jay reminded them of their conversation about tithing and how their willingness to help others was a reflection of God's love in action through them.

He told them that when they gave of their time, energy, and kindness, they were doing something far greater than earning money they were building character and sowing seeds of faith in their neighborhood.

Mekhi and Micah smiled proudly. They realized they hadn't just cut grass that week they had made a difference. Their hearts were full, not because of what they earned, but because of the joy that comes from giving. They decided to tithe part of their earnings, just as their father had taught them, returning thanks to God for His blessings and the opportunity to serve.

That summer, they learned one of life's most powerful truths: when you give freely, God multiplies both the blessing and the joy.

Reflection of the Day

_____

_____

_____

_____

_____

_____

_____

_____

_____

_____

_____

_____

_____

_____

Day Eight ~ The Power of Self-Control

Scripture

> *"But the fruit of the Spirit is love, joy,*
> *peace, patience, kindness, goodness,*
> *faithfulness, gentleness, and self-control.*
> *Against such things there is no law."*
> *Galatians 5:22–23 (KJV)*

Prayer

Father,

Today, we come before You asking for patience, wisdom, and guidance for Mekhi, and Micah. Lord, we know that in their frustration over a simple video game, emotions ran high and tempers took over. Mekhi's anger led him to act without self-control, and both of them later realized their mistake, humbly saying, *"Bro, that was stupid."*

We thank You, Father, for their repentant hearts and for the understanding that followed. You are gracious to teach us even through our failures.

Your Word reminds me,

"Whoever is patient has great understanding,
but one who is quick-tempered displays folly." Proverbs 14:29

Help Micah and Mekhi to grow in patience and self-control. Teach them to pause, breathe, and seek peace when anger rises. Let them respond with gentleness and wisdom rather than frustration or pride.

Father, bring healing to their hearts and to their relationship. May this experience become a steppingstone toward maturity rather than a source of shame. Remind them that mistakes can be redeemed when we learn from them and allow Your Spirit to shape us.

We ask that You fill their hearts with Your peace and strengthen their bond as brothers. May they always choose understanding over anger and love over pride.

In Jesus' Name, Amen.

Reflection: No More TV

It started out like any other day. Mekhi, and Micah were deep into their favorite basketball video game, fully immersed in the competition. As usual, the stakes felt high pride, bragging rights, and brotherly rivalry all on the line.

Micah, who had a knack for the game, was winning more often than not. Mekhi, frustrated by his losses, began to show signs of irritation. Micah's playful teasing, meant in good fun, only added fuel to the fire.

Before long, words turned into tension, and tension turned into anger. In a sudden burst of frustration, Mekhi stood up and slammed his hand against the television screen. A sharp *crack* echoed through the room as the screen shattered and the game instantly went dark.

For a moment, there was complete silence. Micah stood frozen, staring at the broken TV in disbelief. Mekhi's face shifted from anger to shock and regret as the reality of what he'd done sank in.

Neither of them spoke. The room that had been filled with laughter and noise moments earlier was now heavy with guilt and sadness. Mekhi whispered, *"That was stupid,"* his voice soft and full of remorse.

Micah, though upset, felt compassion for his brother. He knew Mekhi's anger wasn't really about the game it was about losing control. Instead of responding with more anger, Micah remembered the words of ***James 1:19***

> **"Everyone should be quick to listen, slow to speak, and slow to become angry."**

He took a deep breath and simply said, "It's okay, bro. We'll figure it out."

Mekhi nodded silently, his eyes full of tears. In that moment, he thought about ***Galatians 5:22–23*** about the fruit of the Spirit and how love, peace, and self-control were what he wanted to reflect, not anger or regret.

Later, Jay sat with the Twinz to talk about what happened. He reminded them that self-control is one of the greatest strengths a person can have and that real maturity means choosing peace over pride.

The broken TV eventually got replaced, but the lesson remained. Mekhi and Micah learned that anger, if left unchecked, can destroy more than just objects it can damage relationships. But they also discovered that humility, forgiveness, and love have the power to repair what was broken.

That day wasn't about losing a game; it was about gaining wisdom. Through it all, God's gentle hand turned a moment of frustration into a lesson of grace reminding them both that true strength is found not in winning, but in *self-control*.

Reflection of the Day:

_____

_____

_____

_____

_____

_____

_____

_____

_____

_____

_____

_____

_____

_____

Day Nine ~ Defender of the Fatherless

Scripture

> *"Defend the poor and fatherless: do justice to the afflicted and needy." Psalm 82:3 (KJV)*

Prayer

Father,

You are the Defender of the weak and the Father to the fatherless. You call us not only to care for ourselves and those we know, but to stand for justice and mercy for others especially the vulnerable and the voiceless.

Today, I lift up every foster and adoptive child, Your precious gifts, into Your loving care and protection.

Lord, defend them from all forms of harm verbal, emotional, or physical. Shield them from abuse, neglect, and rejection. Surround them with Your angels, and grant them safety, peace, and stability in their homes, schools, and communities.

Father, I pray for justice on behalf of every child who has experienced hardship or injustice. Let Your righteous hand intervene in their situations, bringing healing where there is pain, restoration where there is loss, and hope where there has been despair.

Grant wisdom and discernment to all who oversee their care; social workers, judges, lawyers, educators, caregivers, and advocates. Guide them to make decisions that reflect Your heart and prioritize the best interests of every child entrusted to them.

Jesus, comfort the hearts of children who feel abandoned, overlooked, or misunderstood. Remind them that they are never alone and that Your love for them is everlasting. Help them to find their identity, purpose, and security in You.

Father, strengthen foster and adoptive parents with patience, compassion, and perseverance. Equip them with everything they need spiritually, emotionally, and financially to provide nurturing homes that reflect Your love.

Open doors of wisdom and courage for lawmakers and policymakers. Stir their hearts to enact laws that protect, uplift, and support foster and adoptive children. Improve systems and structures so that no child is left unseen or unheard.

Raise up mentors, advocates, and role models who will speak life, value, and encouragement into the hearts of foster and adoptive children. Help them see their infinite worth and the beautiful future You have designed for them.

Father, may Your love shine brightly through every person who interacts with these precious lives. Let them experience Your love, joy, and peace in abundance through the hands and hearts of those who care for them.

Finally, Father, we entrust every foster and adoptive child into Your capable, loving hands, knowing that You are their ultimate Defender, Provider, and Protector.

We thank You in advance for hearing and answering our prayer.

In Jesus' Name, Amen.

Reflection: The Hidden Friend

There are moments when God's compassion shows up in unexpected ways and sometimes, it shows up through our children.

I'll never forget the day we discovered that Micah and Mekhi had been hiding a friend in our basement. It was their favorite hangout spot filled with weights, workout gear, and that unmistakable energy of teenage life. For two days, Jay and I noticed they were taking extra food downstairs, and we couldn't quite figure out why. It wasn't until Mekhi finally came clean that the truth came to light.

Their friend, another young boy from the neighborhood, had been put out of his home. With nowhere else to go, he'd come to the only place he felt safe our house. And without saying a word to us, Micah and Mekhi had quietly taken it upon themselves to feed him, shelter him, and protect him.

At first, I didn't know whether to be upset or amazed. My motherly instincts kicked in, worrying about safety, boundaries, and rules. But as I looked at Mekhi's, I saw something else compassion. I saw the heart of a child who simply couldn't bear to see a friend cold or hungry, especially because they had been him before.

In that moment, I realized that God was working through them. They had done what ***Psalm 82:3*** commands: ***"Defend the poor and fatherless; do justice to the afflicted and needy."*** Their actions weren't rebellious, they were righteous. They saw a need and acted with love, even when they didn't have all the answers.

We sat down together that night and talked about what had happened. We explained the importance of telling us sooner, so we could help properly but I also made sure to tell them how proud I was. Proud that their hearts were tender enough to care. Proud that, without realizing it, they had reflected the very character of God the Defender of the Fatherless.

That night, we reached out to help their friend; first by contacting his mother. And as I watched our boys carry down blankets, Gatorade, and snacks, I realized something profound; they weren't just lifting weights in that basement they were learning the weight of responsibility, empathy, and godly love.

Sometimes, defending the "fatherless" doesn't look like grand gestures or perfect plans. Sometimes, it looks like two young boys sneaking food into a basement because their hearts refused to let someone face the night alone.

Reflection of the Day

_____

_____

_____

_____

_____

_____

_____

_____

_____

_____

_____

_____

_____

_____

Day Ten ~ Building One Another Up

Scripture

> *"Wherefore comfort yourselves together,*
> *and edify one another, even as also ye do."*
> *1 Thessalonians 5:11 (KJV)*

Prayer

Father,

We come before You today, lifting up every foster and adoptive family who has answered Your call to love and care for the precious gifts You have entrusted to them. Lord, pour out Your abundant blessings upon them. Fill their hearts with wisdom, patience, and unwavering love that reflects Your own.

You know the unique challenges they face and the weight they often carry. Strengthen them, Lord, in moments of doubt, weariness, and uncertainty. Remind them that Your strength is made perfect in weakness, and that You are present in every moment guiding, sustaining, and empowering them to continue the work You've called them to do.

Surround these families with a strong community of support people who will encourage one another, share burdens, and celebrate victories together. Let them comfort and build one another up, just as Your Word instructs in *1 Thessalonians 5:11*. May their fellowship be rooted in love, unity, and the grace that comes only from You.

Grant them courage to persevere when the journey feels long and exhausting. Restore their joy as they begin to see the fruit of their faith and labor. Let their homes be havens of peace, safety, and unconditional love places where every child in their care can grow, heal, and thrive under Your watchful eye.

We ask for unity among all foster and adoptive families, that they may shine as lights of hope to the world living testimonies of Your faithfulness, compassion, and redemptive power. May their example reveal the beauty of selfless love and the strength found in obedience to Your call.

And Father, remind us all that You are the ultimate Parent the perfect Father who adopts us into Your eternal family. Help us to mirror that same love in every interaction and relationship we have.

In Jesus' Name, Amen.

Reflection: A Prayer Partner Named Mrs. Ann

When I met Ann, I quickly realized that God had sent her into my life for a very special reason. She was an adoptive parent too someone who understood, in ways few others could, the unique joys and challenges that come with fostering and adoption.

Our conversations flowed easily from the very beginning. There was no need to explain the emotions that come with loving children who have experienced pain, or the weight of advocating for their needs in a system that often overlooks them. Ann simply understood.

We often laughed about the chaos that seemed to follow us both homework battles, long nights of worry, and those moments of deep, unexpected joy that reminded us why we said yes to this calling in the first place. But more than anything, we prayed.

Ann became not just a friend, but a prayer partner. On the days when I felt discouraged or drained, she was the one who would text a simple, "Let's pray." Sometimes we'd call and pray right over the phone interceding for our children, for one another, and for the families walking a similar road. Other times we'd meet for coffee, share tears, and end our time together in prayer, hands clasped, hearts lifted.

There was something sacred about having someone who didn't just listen but truly carried the burden alongside me in prayer. Ann reminded me that fostering and adoption were never meant to be journeys walked alone. God, in His wisdom, provides people brothers and sisters in Christ who understand, encourage, and strengthen us when our own strength runs low.

Through our friendship, I learned that the real beauty of community isn't found in perfection but in shared purpose. We didn't have all the answers, but we knew the One who did. Together, we learned to lean on His promises and to remind each other of His faithfulness.

Ann's friendship became one of the greatest gifts of my fostering and adoption journey. She was a mirror of God's love steady, patient, and prayerful. And though our lives were full of challenges, we both knew that prayer made the load lighter, the hope brighter, and the journey sweeter.

Even now, I thank God for Ann a faithful friend, a prayer warrior, and a reminder that God often sends His comfort wrapped in the form of another person who simply understands.

Reflection of the Day

Day Eleven ~ Serving Without Complaint

Scripture

> *"Do all things without murmurings and disputings." Philippians 2:14 (KJV)*

Prayer

Father,

We come before You with hearts full of gratitude for the privilege of serving as foster and adoptive parents. Thank You for entrusting us with this sacred responsibility to love, guide, and nurture the precious gifts You have placed in our care.

Lord, You have called us to look beyond our own interests and to consider the needs of others, especially the children You've blessed us to serve. Help us to do so with humility, compassion, and selflessness.

Grant us the grace to care for these children without murmuring or complaining, even in moments of exhaustion or challenge. Teach us to see every situation through Your eyes an opportunity to serve, to sow love, and to reflect Your heart.

Father, we ask for patience and wisdom as we guide the children in our home **(call the name of your foster/adopted child)** through their own unique journeys. Help us to understand their stories, their fears, and their emotions, so that we can provide the stability, reassurance, and encouragement they need to thrive.

Give us insight into their backgrounds and experiences, that we might respond with empathy and grace rather than frustration or judgment. May our words and actions consistently reflect Your unconditional love, even when the road feels long or difficult.

Father, we lift each child before You, knowing that You have written a divine plan and purpose for their lives. Fill them with Your peace in the midst of uncertainty, Your joy in moments of sorrow, and Your healing where there has been pain. Surround them with Your presence and remind them daily that they are loved, chosen, and never forgotten.

Thank You, Lord, for the opportunity to make an impact in their lives. May our home be a sanctuary of love, acceptance, and support a place where they can grow, heal, and blossom into all You created them to be.

Guide us to be faithful stewards of Your grace, sharing Your love not only with these children, but with every life that enters our doors. May we serve joyfully, love deeply, and parent in a way that honors You in all things.

In Jesus' Name, Amen.

Reflection: A Thorn, a Lesson, and Grace

There came a season when I found myself weary emotionally, mentally, and spiritually. The Twinz' behavior had reached a breaking point. They were skipping school, running away, and testing every limit I had set as both a parent and a person.

There were days when I wanted to give up. I felt drained and discouraged, wondering if I was truly equipped for the journey of foster and adoptive parenting. I loved them deeply, but love didn't erase the exhaustion or the pain of seeing them struggle to make good choices.

One evening, after yet another long day of frustration, I caught myself complaining to God and to myself. I poured out every grievance, every disappointment, every "why me?" moment. In the middle of my venting, I suddenly grew quiet. Conviction settled over my heart, and I whispered, "Lord, forgive me."

God reminded me that these were His sons before they were mine, and that He had trusted me not because I was perfect, but because I was willing. He brought to my mind *2 Corinthians 12:7-9*, where Paul actually speaks of his own struggle:

"There was given to me a thorn in the flesh…
Three times I pleaded with the Lord to take it away from me.
But He said to me, 'My grace is sufficient for thee, for My strength is made perfect in weakness.'"

In that moment, I realized that my "thorn" wasn't punishment it was purpose. The challenge wasn't meant to destroy me, but to remind me of my need for God's grace.

Later that night, I overheard Jay talking with the Twinz after another misstep. His tone was calm, his words filled with love and truth. The boys were quiet, listening intently, remorseful for what they had done. It struck me beneath their mistakes, they wanted to do better. They were battling pain and confusion I couldn't always see, but their hearts still longed to grow, and to grow according to God's purpose for their lives.

That realization softened me. Complaining wouldn't help them heal, but compassion could. I began praying differently not "Lord, change them," but "Lord, change me while You work on them."

It wasn't easy. There were still difficult days. But over time, I learned to see progress instead of problems, grace instead of guilt. God used those moments to refine not only the Twinz, but me to remind me that love without patience is incomplete, and that growth often looks messy before it bears fruit.

Through tears, prayer, and many second chances, I learned that parenting especially in foster and adoption isn't about perfection. It's about presence. And in my weakest moments, His grace truly was sufficient.

Reflection of the Day

_____

_____

_____

_____

_____

_____

_____

_____

_____

_____

_____

_____

_____

Day Twelve ~ God Is With You Always

Scripture

> *"Be strong and courageous, do not be afraid or tremble at them,*
> *for the Lord your God is the one who goes with you.*
> *He will not fail you nor forsake you."*
> *Deuteronomy 31:6 (KJV)*

Prayer

Father,

We come before You with hearts full of gratitude for the precious children You have entrusted to our care. Just as You promised in *Deuteronomy 31:6*, we take comfort in knowing that You go with us in every circumstance, and that You will never leave us nor forsake us.

Father, this truth remains steadfast today. Through every challenge, every victory, every tear, and every breakthrough You have been there. You never left us. You never failed us.

We pray now for strength, courage, and wisdom as we continue walking alongside the children You've given us *(call the name of your foster/adopted child)*. Help us to be sources of love, stability, and security, resting in the assurance that You are our ultimate refuge and strength.

Grant us patience, Lord, to navigate the uncertainties of each day. Remind us that even when we feel weary, Your grace is sufficient and Your presence is constant.

Father, we lift these children to You, fully confident that their lives are held safely in Your hands. Grant them peace in moments of transition, hope for their future, and healing for every hurt that lingers from the past. Let them feel Your presence surrounding them comforting, guiding, and assuring them that they are deeply loved and created with a divine purpose by the One who gives all purpose.

Father, guide us as we advocate for them. Give us discernment to make wise decisions on their behalf, and compassion to nurture their hearts with understanding and grace. Fill us with Your love so completely that it overflows into every interaction, allowing them to experience *Your* love through *our* actions, words, and care.

Thank You, Father, for the privilege of being part of their story for trusting us to help shape their path and point them toward You. May our home always be a sanctuary of peace, joy, and belonging, reflecting Your grace and mercy in every corner.

Help us to plant seeds of faith, hope, and resilience in their hearts, seeds that will take root and grow into a legacy that brings glory to Your name.

In Jesus' Name, Amen.

Reflection: Advocating for the Twinz

Advocacy became one of the most important parts of our journey with Mekhi and Micah. Both boys had Individualized Education Programs (IEPs) to help support their unique learning needs. As parents, Jay and I quickly learned that our role wasn't just to love them at home it was also to make sure that every promise, every goal, and every plan outlined for them in the classroom was actually being fulfilled.

There were days when it felt like a full-time mission phone calls, meetings, and countless follow-ups but we knew that staying involved was the only way to ensure our boys received what they needed to thrive. Whenever something didn't seem right or when we sensed the plan wasn't being followed as it should, Jay and I were immediately at the school.

We didn't go to argue; we went to *advocate*. We went as parents determined to make sure that the gifts God had entrusted to us were seen, supported, and valued. It wasn't about confrontation it was about collaboration, about keeping everyone accountable for the future of two young men whose potential we refused to let slip through the cracks.

Each meeting reminded me that advocacy is a form of love in action. It meant showing up again and again because our children needed to know that their voices mattered and that their parents would stand with them no matter what.

There were times when it was exhausting, but even then, God's grace showed up in the details. Teachers began to notice the boys' progress, and small victories began to build over time. It wasn't always easy, but each time we saw even the slightest improvement a better grade, a positive report, or a moment of confidence it made every meeting, every prayer, and every bit of persistence worthwhile.

I often think of ***Deuteronomy 31:6***, ***"Be strong and courageous...for the Lord your God is the one who goes with you."*** This Scripture carried us through those long days of advocating, reminding us that we weren't standing alone. God was with us in every conference room, every difficult conversation, and every breakthrough moment.

Looking back, I realize that advocacy is not just about fighting for educational needs it's about fighting for destiny. It's about standing in the gap until your children can stand on their own. And in every step of that journey, God remained faithful never leaving, never forsaking, and always guiding us toward what was best for Mekhi and Micah.

Reflection of the Day

_____

_____

_____

_____

_____

_____

_____

_____

_____

_____

_____

_____

_____

_____

_____

Day Thirteen ~ Trust That There Will Always Be Enough

Scripture

> *"For I was an hungred, and ye gave me meat:*
> *I was thirsty, and ye gave me drink:*
> *I was a stranger, and ye took me in:*
> *Naked, and ye clothed me:*
> *I was sick, and ye visited me:*
> *I was in prison, and ye came unto me."*
> *Matthew 25:35–36 (KJV)*

Prayer

Father,

We come before You with hearts full of gratitude for the privilege of serving as foster and adoptive parents, following the example set forth in *Matthew 25:35–36*. You have called us to feed the hungry, welcome the stranger, and care for those in need. Thank You for entrusting us with these precious gifts **(call the name of your foster/adopted child)** who are seeking love, stability, and hope for their future.

Father, we lift each child in our care to You, asking that You meet their every need, just as Your Word promises in *Philippians 4:19*

> *"And my God shall supply every need of yours according to His riches in glory by Christ Jesus."*

Grant them comfort in moments of uncertainty, healing from past wounds, and strength to face each new day with courage and resilience.

May our home be a place where they experience Your unconditional love and acceptance. Help us to provide both physical and spiritual nourishment as we share meals, laughter, and life together. Let our words and actions reflect Your kindness, compassion, and care in all that we do.

Give us wisdom, patience, and discernment as we navigate the joys and challenges of parenting. Teach us how to advocate for our children faithfully, ensuring that their voices are heard and their needs are met. Equip us to be a beacon of hope and stability in their lives, always pointing them back to You.

Thank You, Father, for the privilege of being vessels of Your love and grace. May we continue to serve with joy and humility, knowing that in caring for these children, we are serving You.

In Jesus' Name, Amen.

Reflection: Why Are You Hiding Food?

For a while, it was a mystery. The food in our house kept disappearing, and I couldn't figure out why. At first, I assumed the boys were sneaking snacks after dinner typical child mischief but something about it didn't add up.

Eventually, the truth came to light. One afternoon, while helping **Mekhi** and **Micah** clean their room, I found their secret stash. Under the bed, inside pillowcases, and tucked away in corners of the closet were packages of food chips, cookies, snack cakes, Jell-O cups, even a forgotten piece of cheese that had long since turned green. Some wrappers were empty, others still sealed, all carefully hidden away.

In that moment, it hit me. The Twinz weren't being defiant they were afraid. Somewhere deep inside, they carried the memory of not having enough. They weren't hoarding out of greed; they were holding on to security. Saving food was their way of making sure they wouldn't go hungry again.

I sat them down and explained that they didn't have to hide food anymore. I told them that in our house, there would always be enough for everyone. There was no need to store snacks in secret because we would always make sure their needs were met. We talked about trust, about how food was meant to be shared and enjoyed together, not hidden away in fear.

As their hearts began to heal, the secret stashes disappeared. Slowly, they learned to trust that there would always be a next meal, always enough to go around, and always someone to care for them.

That simple experience reminded me of how God deals with us. So often, we hold on tightly to things afraid there won't be enough love, provision, or grace for tomorrow. But God gently reminds us that He is our Provider. Just as He said in *Philippians 4:19*, He will supply every need according to His riches in glory.

Through the Twinz, I learned that love, consistency, and patience can heal even the deepest fears. And like them, I continue to learn that when we truly trust our Father, we no longer need to hide anything away because in His house, there will always be enough.

Reflection of the Day

_____

_____

_____

_____

_____

_____

_____

_____

_____

_____

_____

_____

_____

_____

_____

Day Fourteen ~ Love in Action

Scripture

> *"My little children, let us not love in word, neither in tongue;*
> *but in deed and in truth." 1 John 3:18 (KJV)*

Prayer

Father,

We come before You with hearts open to Your love and guidance, inspired by the words of *1 John 3:18*. You have called us to love not merely through words or speech, but through our actions and in truth. Thank You for the privilege of serving as foster and adoptive parents living out Your love daily in tangible ways as we care for the precious gifts You have entrusted to us.

Father, help us to demonstrate Your love to each child *(call the name of your foster/adopted child)* in our home. May our actions speak louder than our words, revealing kindness, patience, forgiveness, and unconditional acceptance. Grant us the wisdom and sensitivity to meet their physical, emotional, and spiritual needs.

Comfort their hearts, Lord, in times of fear or uncertainty. Heal the wounds of their past and restore their hope for the future. May they feel Your presence surrounding them every day bringing peace, safety, and assurance that they are deeply loved by You.

Father, we ask for strength and perseverance as we navigate the complexities of the foster care journey and the responsibilities of adoption. When the process feels overwhelming, remind us that Your grace is sufficient and that You have equipped us for this calling.

Grant us resilience in moments of trial and joy in moments of progress. Help us to celebrate even the smallest victories as signs of Your faithfulness at work in their lives and ours.

Thank You, Father, for the honor of making a lasting impact in these young lives. May our home be a refuge of safety, growth, and love a place where Your light shines brightly through our words, actions, and attitudes.

Teach us to love genuinely and selflessly, reflecting Your heart to all who enter our home. Let every embrace, every word of encouragement, and every act of care testify of Your goodness and truth.

In Jesus' Name, Amen.

Reflection: Love in Action and The Father's Day Plaque

The Twinz were ten years old when they reminded me what real love in action looks like. I had just purchased new supplies to create a jewelry display case for my Paparazzi business a project I was excited to begin. Everything was neatly organized and set aside, ready for me to get started.

But a few days later, I noticed the supplies were missing. My first thought, as any parent might understand, was a mix of confusion and frustration. "Where did all my materials go?" I wondered.

Then I found them scattered across the kitchen table, covered in glue, paint, and glitter. And right in the center of all that awesome chaos were Mekhi and Micah, proudly working on something they didn't want me to see just yet.

When they finally revealed their project, I couldn't help but smile. Using the very supplies I had set aside for my own work, the Twinz had created a homemade Father's Day plaque for Jay. It wasn't perfect the lines weren't straight, the paint was smudged, and the glue hadn't quite dried but it was beautiful.

They had poured their little hearts into it. Every letter, every crooked detail, every fingerprint of paint was a reflection of their love. In that moment, I couldn't be upset not even a little. They had taken what they had and used it to show love in the purest way possible.

As I looked at their creation, *1 John 3:18* came to life before my eyes:

> *"My little children, let us not love in word, neither in tongue; but in deed and in truth."*

The plaque wasn't about perfection it was about *heart*. The Twinz didn't just talk about how much they loved their dad; they showed it through their actions.

Later that day, when they presented it to Jay, the joy on his face said it all. He didn't see flaws or mistakes; he saw *love*. And I realized that God sees us much the same way. When we act out of love no matter how imperfectly He receives it with joy, because He looks at the heart behind the effort.

That day, the Twinz taught me something invaluable: true love doesn't always come wrapped in perfection or polish. Sometimes, it's found in sticky glue, smudged paint, and the hands of two little boys trying their best to honor their father. And in those small, heartfelt gestures, God's love shines the brightest.

Reflection of the Day

_____

_____

_____

_____

_____

_____

_____

_____

_____

_____

_____

_____

_____

_____

Day Fifteen ~ Yet Will I Trust Him

Scripture

> *"Though he slay me, yet will I hope in him;*
> *I will surely defend my ways to his face."*
> *Job 13:15 (KJV)*

Prayer

Father,

Having had to grieve the loss of two sons Mekhi (January 2023), and Micah (May 2024) within the span of one year is a pain beyond what I could ever have imagined. My heart aches in ways words can hardly describe. Yet, even in the depths of sorrow, I still choose to thank You. You have been faithful through every tear, every long night, and every moment when I thought I couldn't go on.

Lord, I thank You for the precious time we had with Mekhi and Micah. Though their time here was far too short, we cherish every memory, every laugh, and every conversation. Thank You for the bonds we formed, the love they gave, and the joy they brought into our lives.

Those moments are treasures we will carry in our hearts forever.

We also thank You for the challenges we've faced along the way. As James reminds us, we are to count it all joy when we encounter trials of many kinds. Though it is hard to understand why our sons were taken from us, we trust that You are using our pain for a greater purpose. You are strengthening our faith, deepening our dependence on You, and teaching us to hold onto Your promises especially when life feels unbearable, and out of our control.

Thank You for continuing to cover and protect our children and grandchildren JT, Juanita, Jessika, Katyce, Romesha, Robert, Brittany, Chesarae, Jeremiah, Isaiah, Jaziah, Aniah, Aden, Joy, Dorae, and Jordan; and our entire family as we navigate our lives without the Twinz. May Your peace, which surpasses all understanding, guard our hearts and minds. Let us continue to sense Your presence with us, even in our deepest sorrow.

Father, we are especially grateful for their father, who served as a steady voice of faith in their lives drawing them closer to You. Thank You for the rededication of Mekhi's heart before his passing and for Jay's faithful love and guidance that helped point our Twinz toward

You. We pray that Mekhi and Micah's legacy lives on through the faith they found in You and that the seeds planted in their hearts will bear fruit for generations to come to those who genuinely knew them.

Your Word promises that You are near to the brokenhearted and that You save those who are crushed in spirit. As we continue to grieve, wrap us in Your loving arms. Heal our broken hearts and help us walk forward in faith, confident that our sons are safe in Your eternal embrace.

We trust in Your sovereignty even when we cannot understand. We surrender our pain to You and declare that You are still good, even in our grief. Thank You for being our refuge and strength—a very present help in our time of need.

We will continue to praise You, Father, because You are worthy. And we hold fast to the hope that one day, we will be reunited with Mekhi and Micah in Your perfect, eternal kingdom.

In Jesus' Name, Amen.

Reflection: A Testimony of Faith in the Midst of Grief

On January 25, 2023, our lives were changed forever. Our son, Mekhi James Harrison, was taken from us by gun violence by someone he had once called his childhood best friend. In an instant, everything shattered.

Mekhi was not perfect none of us are, but he was perfect in God's eyes. Just days earlier, he had rededicated his life to Christ, a moment that now serves as a beacon of hope in the midst of our pain.

I will never forget the call from my daughter, Romesha. Her voice trembled as she asked, "Mom, why does it say, 'Rest in Peace' on Mekhi's Instagram page?" My heart dropped. I called my husband immediately, though I can't recall if he answered. I left work and drove straight to the church, knowing somehow that I would find him there.

When I turned into the parking lot and saw two police cars waiting, my body went numb. And then I saw Jay's face broken, devastated, holding a pain I had never seen before. We embraced, and in that moment, though shattered, I felt God holding us together.

The grief was crushing. I wept not only for Mekhi, but for his twin brother, Micah. I couldn't comprehend how we would move forward. Mekhi had just renewed his faith; he was finding his way. It wasn't supposed to end this way. In the midst of the pain we still trusted God.

But as we were still trying to recover from the heartbreak of Mekhi's death, another devastating blow came. On May 19, 2024, Micah drowned in the Chinook River while visiting Indiana with his biological family. On this particular day Micah was swimming in a restricted area with friends that he had met while there, and in one tragic moment, he too was gone. But in the midst of another devastating blow to our family we still trusted God.

Losing both of our boys felt unbearable like the air had been taken from our lungs. Yet, even in our despair, we knew God was still with us. Our faith, though tested beyond measure, did not break. Instead, it deepened.

We held onto ***Job 13:15, "Though He slay me, yet will I trust Him."*** Those words became like an anchor. We didn't understand, but we chose to trust.

Through every tear, every sleepless night, every aching silence, God sustained us. We saw His strength in the prayers of others, His comfort in moments of stillness, and His love in the memories that refused to fade.

We believe with all our hearts that our sons are now with the Lord. Mekhi, redeemed and restored, and Micah, gentle and full of love both resting in His eternal presence. The grief remained, but so does our hope.

Their deaths have taught me that God's comfort is stronger than any storm, His peace deeper than any pain, and His love greater than death itself.

Our faith has been refined in fire. It is unshaken, unmovable, and rooted in the truth that God is still good. We will continue to honor Mekhi and Micah by living with faith, by serving others, and by trusting that their lives and even their deaths have purpose in God's eternal plan.

Though we mourn deeply, we also rejoice. For one day, we will see them again. And until that day, we will continue to praise the God who gives, who sustains, and who promises that His love never ends.

Reflection of the Day

_____

_____

_____

_____

_____

_____

_____

_____

_____

_____

_____

_____

_____

Day 16 ~ Choosing the Right Friends

Scripture

> *"Walk with the wise and become wise,*
> *for a companion of fools suffers harm."*
> *Proverbs 13:20 (KJV)*

Prayer

Father,

We come before You today, lifting up Mekhi and Micah as they learn to choose friends who will encourage them to walk in wisdom and draw closer to You. Lord, we know that the company they keep will shape their hearts, their choices, and their futures. We ask for Your divine guidance as they navigate these relationships.

Surround them, Father, with friends who love You, who live with integrity, and who honor their parents. May they build friendships with those who strengthen their faith rather than weaken it friends who speak truth, offer encouragement, and reflect Your love in all they do.

Your Word in *Proverbs 13:20* reminds us that those who walk with the wise become wise, but those who keep company with fools will suffer harm. We ask that

You help Mekhi and Micah discern the difference between wisdom and foolishness. Protect them from harmful influences and from relationships that would lead them away from their purpose.

Give them eyes to recognize genuine friendship and the courage to walk away from people or situations that dishonor You. May they always find strength in Your Word and wisdom in their choices.

We trust in Your plan for their lives, Lord. Lead them into divine connections that help them grow in character, faith, and understanding. May every friendship they form glorify You and align with the destiny You've designed for them.

In Jesus' Name, Amen.

Reflection: Who Are Your Friends?

As Mekhi and Micah grew older, I began to notice changes in the friends they chose. The young men they surrounded themselves with no longer reflected the values we had worked so hard to instill in them. Some of these friends were involved in behaviors that broke my heart such as robbing, smoking marijuana, and using profanity as if it were normal conversation.

It was painful to watch. Jay and I had poured so much love, teaching, and prayer into our sons, and yet their choices began to drift in the opposite direction of everything we had taught them. There were moments I wondered if the lessons of integrity, respect, and faith had somehow been forgotten.

But even in my grief, I chose to believe that the Word was tucked away inside of them. Deep in my heart, I held onto the truth that the seeds we had planted would one day take root again. I trusted that the Word of God, which had been spoken over their lives since childhood, would not return void.

There were nights I cried and prayed, asking God to open their eyes to show them the difference between the friends who would lift them up and those who would pull them down. I prayed that they would remember who they were and Whose they were, and that the voice of truth within them would be louder than the noises around them.

As a parent, there are few things harder than watching your children struggle with choices you can't control. But I learned that my role wasn't to fix everything it was to pray through everything.

I prayed with faith that the same God who called them into our lives would also call them back to the path of righteousness. And even when I couldn't see it, I trusted that He was working in ways I didn't understand placing the right people, the right situations, and the right moments to remind the Twinz of His truth and purpose for their lives.

Today, I continue to believe that the foundation we built faith, family, and love will always rise above the noise. Because God's Word never fades, and His promises never fail.

Reflection of the Day:

_____

_____

_____

_____

_____

_____

_____

_____

_____

_____

_____

_____

_____

Day Seventeen ~ Training Up a Child

Scripture

> *"Train up a child in the way he should go: and when he is old, he will not depart from it." Proverbs 22:6 (KJV)*

Prayer

Father,

We come before You with hearts full of gratitude for the privilege of serving as a foster and adoptive family, guided by the truth of ***Proverbs 22:6 "Train up a child in the way he should go, and when he is old, he will not depart from it."*** Thank You for entrusting us with the Twinz precious gifts, each one uniquely designed and lovingly created by You.

Lord, we ask for Your guidance and wisdom as we nurture and care for these Mekhi, and Micah in our home. Help us to provide a loving, stable environment where they can grow physically, emotionally, and spiritually. Grant us patience when challenges arise and joy when we celebrate their victories.

Father, we ask for Your divine protection over every child You have placed in our care. Shield them from harm, both seen and unseen. Surround them with Your angels and let Your peace dwell richly in their hearts. May they always feel secure, valued, and deeply loved not only by us, but by You, their Heavenly Father.

We also lift up the birth families of children who have been placed in foster homes and adoptive homes. Lord, bring healing where there is pain, reconciliation where there is separation, and restoration where there is loss. Let Your mercy and wisdom guide them, and may Your grace touch every part of their lives.

Thank You, Father, for the sacred opportunity to be part of Your redemptive work in the lives of Your children. Help us to faithfully fulfill Your calling to love, guide, and train them according to Your Word. May our home be a place where Your presence is evident, Your peace abides, and Your love shines through all who enter.

We trust that every seed of faith, every lesson taught, and every prayer whispered will bear fruit in their future.

In Jesus' Name, Amen.

Reflection: Twinz in Training

Raising Mekhi and Micah according to Scripture has always been a responsibility that Jay and I took to heart very seriously. From the moment they came into our lives, we understood that the foundation we built in their early years would shape the men they would one day become. Our challenge was trying to override their initial start in life; which to be quite honest was overwhelming, but we trusted God anyway.

The Bible gives clear instruction on how to raise children in a way that honors God, and we did our best to live out those principles daily in our home, our ministry, and our community even in seasons of struggle, and noncompliance from our wonderful Twinz.

Proverbs 22:6 tells us, **"Train up a child in the way he should go, and when he is old, he will not depart from it."** We knew that our role as parents wasn't just to correct behavior but to shape character. It meant teaching them to make wise choices, to live with integrity, and to know and love God deeply.

We tried to be intentional teaching them to pray, to respect others, and to cherish God's Word. Whether through bedtime devotions, family discussions, or modeling faith in everyday moments, we wanted them to see that serving God wasn't just something you say it's something you live.

Ephesians 6:4 reminds us, "Fathers, do not provoke your children to anger, but bring them up in the discipline and instruction of the Lord." Jay and I held tightly to that truth. We wanted discipline to come from a place of love, never frustration. We aimed to correct with compassion and affirm their worth in God's eyes, even when they stumbled.

We weren't perfect parents far from it. But we were committed. Every lesson, every conversation, every prayer was a seed planted with the hope that one day it would grow. And though their journeys were not without challenges, we trust that those seeds of truth, love, and faith will continue to bear fruit in ways that honor God.

Because in the end, training up a child isn't about perfection it's about purpose. It's about trusting that the same God who gave them to us will continue to guide them long after they leave our arms.

Reflection of the Day

_____

_____

_____

_____

_____

_____

_____

_____

_____

_____

_____

_____

_____

_____

Day Eighteen ~ Perfectly Imperfect

Scripture

> *"I praise You because I am fearfully and*
> *wonderfully made;*
> *Your works are wonderful, I know that*
> *full well."*
> *Psalm 139:14 (KJV)*

Prayer

Heavenly Father,

We come before You today seeking Your guidance and strength as we walk the journey of self-acceptance. Lord, we acknowledge that You have created each one of us fearfully and wonderfully, and we thank You for the unique individuals You have made us to be.

Help us, Father, to see ourselves through Your eyes to recognize the beauty, purpose, and value You have placed within us. When doubt, insecurity, or comparison creep in, remind us that we are not defined by others' opinions or by the world's standards, but by Your perfect love.

Heal our hearts from the lies that tell us we are not enough. Teach us to embrace our gifts, personalities, and even our imperfections, knowing that every part of us was designed intentionally by You. Help us to walk confidently in the truth of **Psalm 139:14**, that we are fearfully and wonderfully made, and that Your works including us are indeed wonderful.

In moments of self-doubt, remind us of **Ephesians 2:10:**

> *"For we are God's handiwork, created in Christ Jesus to do good works, which God prepared in advance for us to do."*

Lord, help us trust that You have a plan for our lives that only we can fulfill. When we fall short or make mistakes, may we remember **Romans 8:37**

> *"No, in all these things we are more than conquerors through Him who loved us."*

Father, teach us to find peace in our imperfections, knowing You are always working all things together for our good. Shape us through every experience and remind us that even our flaws can reflect Your glory when surrendered to You.

Thank You for the gift of identity, confidence, and self-acceptance through Christ. May we live authentically, free from fear and comparison, walking boldly in the truth that we are enough because we are Yours.

In Jesus' Name, Amen.

Reflection: The Barber Experiment We Are Perfectly Imperfect

It all started with one bright idea. Micah, always curious and full of confidence, decided one day that he was going to become a barber. His logic was simple; why pay someone else to cut their hair when he could do it himself? After all, he had enough barbershop visits to figure it out how hard could it be?

"Dad," he said with a grin, "you pay $20 for us to get a haircut twice a month. But what if *I* cut our hair? You could pay *me* instead!"

Jay, amused but supportive of Micah's entrepreneurial spirit, chuckled and said, "Alright, Micah let's see what you've got."

That was all the encouragement Micah needed. Armed with his dad's clippers and a newfound sense of purpose, he set up shop right on the front porch. His first client? Of course his twin brother, Mekhi.

Without hesitation, Mekhi sat down, trusting his brother completely. Micah wrapped a sheet around him like a pro, turned on the clippers, and started buzzing away. The sound filled the air, and for a moment, everything seemed to be going according to plan.

Then came the grand finale.

With a triumphant smile, Micah whipped the sheet off Mekhi and proudly announced, "Finished, bro. Pay up!"

But when Mekhi caught his reflection, what stared back was… something else entirely. The haircut was a masterpiece of creative expression patches, uneven lines, and more "texture" than any barber would recommend. It was, in short, unforgettable.

My first instinct was to rush him straight to the barbershop for repairs. But before I could say a word, Mekhi turned to his brother, grinned, and said, "It's okay I'm rocking it Bro. It's the new style." We all burst into laughter.

That moment, standing on the porch with two boys covered in clippings and giggling uncontrollably, became one of my favorites. Because it wasn't really about the haircut, it was about confidence, love, and grace.

Micah's experiment might not have gone as planned, but it revealed something beautiful: the courage to try, to create, and to fail without shame. And Mekhi's willingness to wear his uneven haircut with pride reminded us that perfection isn't the goal joy is.

That day became a lesson in self-acceptance. Life will always have rough edges and uneven lines, but when we choose to embrace who we are, even in our imperfections, we reflect the image of a perfect God who never makes mistakes.

Because sometimes, the "patchy haircut" moments are the ones that remind us most clearly that we are, indeed, fearfully and wonderfully made.

Reflection of the Day

_____

_____

_____

_____

_____

_____

_____

_____

_____

_____

_____

_____

_____

_____

Day Nineteen ~ Resolving with Love

Scripture

> *"Moreover if thy brother shall trespass against thee,*
> *go and tell him his fault between thee and him alone:*
> *if he shall hear thee, thou hast gained thy brother." Matthew 18:15 (KJV)*

Prayer

Father,

We humbly come before You today, grateful for the privilege and responsibility of serving as a Resource Family. We are guided by the principles found in *Matthew 18:15*, which teaches us to address conflict directly and with love. Thank You for entrusting us with these precious gifts each one uniquely created, cherished, and valued in Your sight.

Lord, we lift up to You the relationships within our home. Grant us wisdom and discernment as we navigate the different personalities, needs, and experiences of each child. Help us to communicate with honesty, gentleness, and compassion. When misunderstandings arise, may we handle them with grace and patience, always seeking peace and reconciliation rather than anger or division.

Father, we pray for unity and harmony in our family. Let Your peace reign in our hearts and guide our interactions. Give us patience to truly listen, humility to admit when we are wrong, and grace to extend forgiveness freely. May our home be a refuge of love, where every child feels seen, safe, and respected.

Protect our household, Lord, from discord and disunity. Guard our hearts from bitterness and discouragement. Strengthen our family's bond through Your Spirit, and help us to walk together in love, truth, and understanding.

We ask that You continue to supply our every need spiritually, emotionally, and physically so that we may serve children faithfully. Let our home reflect the heart of Christ: compassionate, forgiving, and full of grace.

Thank You, Father, for the opportunity to nurture and guide the children You've placed in our care. May our words, actions, and attitudes reflect Your Kingdom principles in every situation. Let Your presence be tangible in our home, bringing healing, restoration, and joy to each member of our family.

In Jesus' Name, Amen.

Reflection: The Lakers Hoodie (A Lesson in Forgiveness and Understanding)

It all started over something simple, but meaningful. Micah had saved up his money to buy a special Christmas gift for Jeremiah, his nephew and best friend. He'd picked out a Lakers hoodie, Jeremiah's favorite team, and wrapped it with care, proud that he was able to give something from his own heart. It wasn't just a hoodie; it was a symbol of thoughtfulness and the bond they shared.

But a few days after Christmas, Micah walked into the room and froze. There was Mekhi, wearing that very same Lakers hoodie the one Micah had bought for Jeremiah.

In an instant, frustration filled the air. "Why are you wearing that?" Micah shouted, his voice rising with hurt and anger. "That was for Jeremiah! You knew that!"

Mekhi, caught off guard, looked confused. "I didn't think it was that serious," he said quietly. "I just grabbed it because it was cold."

But for Micah, it *was* just that serious. He stormed off, angry and disappointed. It wasn't about the hoodie alone it was about the effort, the meaning, and the care behind it. His feelings were hurt because what he'd given from his heart had been treated casually by his brother.

Later that evening, I sat down with both Twinz. We talked about what happened not just the argument, but what was behind it. I reminded Micah of *Matthew 18:15*

> *"If your brother trespasses against you, go and tell him his fault between you and him alone; if he shall hear you, you have gained your brother."*

It was a moment to teach both of them about communication and forgiveness.

Micah, still upset, finally said, "It just mattered to me, Mom. I saved hard to buy that for Jeremiah."
And Mekhi, hearing his brother's heart, nodded. "I didn't mean to make you feel that way, bro. I'm sorry. I wasn't thinking."

Micah sighed, the tension slowly leaving the room. "It's okay. Just ask next time, alright?"

What could've turned into a lingering argument became a lesson in love and understanding. Micah learned the importance of expressing his feelings calmly, and Mekhi learned the value of respect and thoughtfulness toward others' efforts.

By the end of the night, the hoodie had found its new owner in Mekhi, and the two of them were laughing again stronger, closer, and reminded that brotherhood means more than being right; it means choosing grace.

That simple moment became a reflection of how God wants us to handle conflict with honesty, humility, and a heart willing to forgive. Because sometimes, the real gift isn't the hoodie it's learning how to love one another through the misunderstandings that come our way.

Reflection of the Day

_____

_____

_____

_____

_____

_____

_____

_____

_____

_____

_____

_____

Day Twenty ~ Laughter in the House

Scripture:
"The city streets will be filled with boys and girls playing there." *Zechariah 8:5*

Prayer:
Father,
Thank You for the beautiful gift of Micah and Mekhi for their laughter, their boundless energy, and the joy they bring to our hearts. Thank You for their playful spirits, the innocence in their giggles, and the pure delight they find in the simple act of play.

Lord, You designed children to have moments of fun, to explore, to jump, to wrestle, and to create. Play is not just enjoyment it's an expression of learning, discovery, and growth. Through these moments, they develop curiosity, confidence, and connection. Thank You, Lord, for giving them the freedom to simply be children safe, loved, and full of wonder.

We ask that You bless Mekhi, and Micah as they continue to play, laugh, and explore. May their time spent in joy strengthen their bond with each other and inspire creativity that reflects Your divine imagination. Let every burst of laughter and every playful moment be a reminder of Your goodness and love.

Lord, we also pray for their emotional, and cognitive growth that through play they learn cooperation, patience, and resilience. May they find joy in the little things and continue to carry childlike wonder wherever life takes them.

Bless their laughter, their games, their fun, and may they always know that You delight in their joy. Surround them with Your protection, wisdom, and peace as they grow into the young men You've created them to be.

In Jesus' Name, Amen

Reflection: Heaven's Echo in Their Laughter

They may not have been playing in the streets, but inside the Twinz' room, the energy was just as wild and joyful. Micah, Mekhi, and Isaiah had turned their space into a world of imagination and laughter. The bean bag once neatly in place had become a wrestling mat and playground all at once.

The sounds of bouncing, tumbling, and laughter filled the room. Before I could even go back for a second check, there came the unmistakable sound of a rip, and suddenly, a sea of tiny white plastic balls poured across the floor. The boys were in absolute heaven! They threw the balls into the air, rolled through them, and laughed so hard that their joy echoed through the house.

Amid the playful chaos, I saw Isaiah's little eyes peeking out from under the pile before he dove back in, laughing uncontrollably as the Twinz pulled him into the fun. Their giggles mingled together, filling the room with life, love, and innocence.

For that moment, time stood still. Their laughter so pure, and unrestrained reminded me that childhood joy is one of God's sweetest gifts. In their play, I saw a reflection of heaven's peace and the simple truth that sometimes, the holiest moments are the ones spent simply being together, happy and free.

Reflection of the Day:

_____

_____

_____

_____

_____

_____

_____

_____

_____

_____

_____

_____

_____

Day Twenty-One ~ The Blessing of Obedience

Scripture

> **"Children, obey your parents in all things: for this is well pleasing unto the Lord."** *Colossians 3:20*

Prayer,

Heavenly Father,

We come before You as Resource Parents grateful for the sacred opportunity to care for, guide, and nurture the precious children You have entrusted to us. Thank You for the instruction found in Your Word, reminding us in Colossians 3:20 that obedience is not merely about following rules, but about living in a way that is pleasing unto You.

Lord, grant us wisdom, patience, and grace as we teach and model obedience. Help us to reflect Your love through our words and actions so that each child sees a glimpse of Your heart in us. May our discipline be firm but compassionate, and our correction always rooted in love and understanding.

Give us discernment, Father, to recognize the unique personalities, needs, and challenges within each child's heart. Help us to guide them with consistency and care, balancing structure with gentleness, and authority with affection. Let our boundaries be rooted in Your truth, teaching them not only to follow us but ultimately to honor You.

We acknowledge that obedience is not always easy for them or for us. In those moments of defiance, frustration, or misunderstanding, help us respond with patience and faith. Remind us that every moment of correction is also a moment of teaching, and that through loving guidance, their hearts are shaped toward righteousness.

May our home be filled with peace and mutual respect a place where children feel safe, valued, and deeply loved. Let laughter dwell within our walls, and may obedience grow not out of fear, but from trust and love.

We commit each child into Your hands, believing that You have a divine purpose for their lives. May they grow in wisdom, character, and faith pleasing You in all that they do and becoming living testimonies of Your grace.

In Jesus' Name, Amen

Reflection: When Obedience Blossomed

It was one of those busy mornings when everything seemed to happen at once. Breakfast dishes still sat in the sink, the sound of the dryer hummed in the background, and the school van would be pulling up any minute. I called upstairs, "Mekhi, and Micah! Let's go it's time to get ready!"

Usually, that announcement was followed by a chorus of questions, playful delays, or the sound of footsteps that moved just a little too slow. But that morning was different. Within seconds, I heard drawers opening, and slamming closed, sneakers sliding on the floor, and laughter as they helped each other find their missing socks.

When they came downstairs shirts tucked in, faces washed, and bookbags in hand I couldn't help but smile. "Wow," I said, surprised but proud, "you listened the first time." Micah grinned and said, "We didn't want to be late, Mom. We remembered what you said yesterday about being prepared." Mekhi nodded in agreement, adding, "And we didn't even argue this time!"

It was a simple act, but it spoke volumes. Their willingness to listen and follow through showed growth a small step of obedience that reflected something much greater taking root in their hearts.

Later that day, as I watched them walk up the steps to the front door, I thought about how obedience isn't always learned through lectures or correction; or even me yelling it's learned through love, consistency, and trust. Mekhi, and Micah had learned that obedience wasn't just about following rules, but about respect, responsibility, and honoring those who care for them.

That morning became a quiet reminder for me, too that just as they are learning to obey, I'm also learning to obey God's gentle voice in my own life. Their obedience became a reflection of His work in all of us a small, shining example of how faith and love shape hearts, one opportunity at a time.

Reflection of the Day

_____

_____

_____

_____

_____

_____

_____

_____

_____

_____

_____

_____

_____

Day Twenty-Two ~ Known by Their Actions

Scripture

> *"Even a child is known by his doings,*
> *whether his work be pure, and whether it*
> *be right." Proverbs 20:11*

Prayer

Gracious Father,
We lift our hearts to You, grateful for the privilege of being Foster Parents to the precious children placed in our care. Your Word in *Proverbs 20:11* reminds us that even a child is known by their actions whether their conduct is pure and right.

Lord, thank You for Your guidance and strength as we strive to be a beacon of light in the lives of our children. Help us to reflect Your truth and love so that they may be inspired to do what is right in Your sight. Grant us wisdom to teach and lead them with patience and understanding, knowing that every word and action has the power to shape their hearts.

When challenges arise and their behavior strays from what is good, help us to love them unconditionally just as You love each of us. May Your compassion flow through us, offering grace and forgiveness as You do. Give us the ability to see beyond their actions to the deeper needs of their hearts, and to respond with Your heart of mercy and care.

Lord, we pray for moments of connection and understanding, where they may glimpse Your love through our example. May our home be a sanctuary where they feel accepted, valued, and encouraged to grow in Your ways.

We entrust these children into Your loving hands, confident that You have a plan and purpose for each of their lives. May they come to know You more deeply through our love, guidance, and faithfulness.

In Jesus' Name I pray, Amen.

Reflection: When Grace Met Grief

There are moments in life that leave a permanent mark on the soul, moments that change everything you thought you knew about faith, parenting, and love. On this particular day I received the call about Mekhi, and Micah being in a stolen vehicle was one of those moments. They were sixteen still boys in so many ways, yet standing on the edge of manhood, making choices that would carry lifelong consequences for each of them.

The words came through the phone like a thunderclap: "They're being chased through the city." My heart raced faster than the sirens that filled the air. As I followed the flow of traffic toward Morton Avenue in Chester, I prayed under my breath, "Lord, please let them be safe."

When I reached the bridge, chaos surrounded me flashing lights, twisted metal, and the unmistakable hush that falls when tragedy has taken its place. A woman I recognized from their school looked at me with tearful eyes and whispered, "It's the Twinz."

My breath left my body. I saw Micah stumble from the wreckage, dazed but alive. But I didn't see Mekhi. When I tried to push through the yellow tape, desperate to reach my boys, an officer stopped me. "Ma'am, this is a crime scene," he said. My voice broke as I replied, "Those are my sons."

They told me Mekhi was already on his way to Crozer Chester Hospital. When I arrived, I was ushered into a room that no parent ever wants to enter. The sight of our son's still, lifeless, unresponsive body was more than I could bear. Anger surged inside me, anger at the reckless decision that led to this moment, anger at the police officers who decided to chase teenagers through the City of Chester at high speeds, and the friends I warned them about. But as I looked at him, anger gave way to something greater, love. Love that no mistake could erase, love that held both grief and grace at the same time.

That day, **Proverbs 20:11** became more than a verse to me it became a mirror. *"Even a child is known by his doings, whether his work be pure, and whether it be right."* My sons were known not just by their mistakes, but by their hearts the laughter, the kindness, the way they loved fiercely and lived loudly, sometimes if not most erratically.

In the days that followed, I came to understand that God doesn't define our children by their failures. He sees the fullness of who they are their struggles, their potential, and their purpose. Mekhi's story didn't end that day on the bridge. His life continues to speak through the lessons of love, forgiveness, and redemption that God has written on our hearts.

Even in the pain, I am reminded that grace still speaks. God's mercy still reaches. And love; love never dies.

Reflection of the Day:

_____

_____

_____

_____

_____

_____

_____

_____

_____

_____

_____

_____

_____

_____

Day Twenty-Three ~ A Father's Compassion

Scripture

> *"As a father has compassion on his children, so the Lord has compassion on those who fear Him." Psalm 103:13*

Prayer:

Heavenly Father,

We come before You with hearts full of gratitude for the privilege of being Resource Parents to the precious children You have entrusted to our care. Your Word in *Psalm 103:13* reminds us that as a father has compassion on his children, so You have compassion on those who revere You.

Lord, grant us grace and guidance as we strive to reflect Your heart of compassion toward these children. Help us to see them through Your eyes with patience, understanding, and unconditional love. Soften our hearts when challenges arise, and give us wisdom to respond with empathy rather than frustration.

May we be a steady source of comfort and strength in their times of need offering a listening ear, a gentle touch, and a spirit that reassures them they are safe and loved. Help us to cultivate an environment where healing can take place, where old wounds are soothed, and where Your peace abides.

When difficult behaviors or moments of weariness test our patience, remind us of the mercy You so freely extend to us. Let that same mercy flow through us as we guide these children, helping them see themselves not through the lens of their struggles, but through the beauty of Your design valued, cherished, and redeemed.

Lord, let our home be a place of refuge and hope a reflection of Your perfect love. Use us to plant seeds of faith and courage in their hearts, and to nurture their belief that they can overcome any obstacle through You.

We surrender ourselves and these children to Your loving care, trusting that Your plan for their lives is good. May Your peace dwell within our home, and may Your presence guide all that we do.

In Jesus' Name we pray, Amen.

Reflection: A Father's Hands of Compassion

Watching Jay care for Mekhi when he finally returned home from the hospital after more than a month was one of the most powerful sights of compassion I have ever witnessed. His body was still fragile, his wounds deep, and the trach in his neck a constant reminder of what we had endured as a family. Yet, in that moment, love spoke louder than pain.

Even in the lingering anger over the choices that had brought us there, Jay's actions reflected a love that could only come from the Father's heart. With steady hands and quiet strength, he cleaned Mekhi's wounds, changed his bandages, and tended to his needs with the same tenderness one might imagine Jesus showing as He healed the broken.

There was something sacred in the way he leaned over his son carefully, patiently, gently. Each touch seemed to say, "I forgive you. I love you. You are still my son." It reminded me of how God tends to our own wounds those seen and unseen when we've made mistakes and gone astray.

In that small bedroom, love became holy. Jay wasn't just caring for our son's injuries; he was ministering to his spirit. It was as though he were tending to the wounds of Christ Himself, as Jesus endured the stripes that would one day bring us all healing.

That day, I saw what **Psalm 103:13** truly means *"As a father has compassion on his children, so the Lord has compassion on those who fear Him."* Compassion isn't just a feeling it's an act of grace, freely given even when pain is still fresh. Through Jay's hands, I saw God's hands. Through his care, I saw redemption. And through it all, I was reminded that love true love heals more than just the body; it restores the soul.

Reflection of the Day:

_____

_____

_____

_____

_____

_____

_____

_____

_____

_____

_____

_____

_____

_____

Day Twenty-Three ~ A Father's Compassion

Scripture:

> *"As a father has compassion on his children, so the Lord has compassion on those who fear Him." Psalm 103:13*

Prayer

Heavenly Father,

We come before You with hearts full of gratitude for the privilege of being Resource Parents to the precious children You have entrusted to our care. Your Word in Psalm 103:13 reminds us that as a father has compassion on his children, so You have compassion on those who revere You.

Lord, grant us grace and guidance as we strive to reflect Your heart of compassion toward these children. Help us to see them through Your eyes with patience, understanding, and unconditional love. Soften our hearts when challenges arise, and give us wisdom to respond with empathy rather than frustration.

May we be a steady source of comfort and strength in their times of need offering a listening ear, a gentle touch, and a spirit that reassures them they are safe and loved. Help us to cultivate an environment where healing can take place, where old wounds are soothed, and where Your peace abides.

When difficult behaviors or moments of weariness test our patience, remind us of the mercy You so freely extend to us. Let that same mercy flow through us as we guide these children, helping them see themselves not through the lens of their struggles, but through the beauty of Your design valued, cherished, and redeemed.

Lord, let our home be a place of refuge and hope a reflection of Your perfect love. Use us to plant seeds of faith and courage in their hearts, and to nurture their belief that they can overcome any obstacle through You.

We surrender ourselves and these children to Your loving care, trusting that Your plan for their lives is good. May Your peace dwell within our home, and may Your presence guide all that we do.

In Jesus' Name we pray, Amen.

Reflection: A Father's Hands of Compassion

Watching Jay care for Mekhi when he finally returned home from the hospital after more than a month was one of the most powerful sights of compassion I have ever witnessed. His body was still fragile, his wounds deep, and the trach in his neck a constant reminder of what we had endured as a family. Yet, in that moment, love spoke louder than pain.

Even in the lingering anger over the choices that had brought us there, Jay's actions reflected a love that could only come from the Father's heart. With steady hands and quiet strength, he cleaned Mekhi's wounds, changed his bandages, and tended to his needs with the same tenderness one might imagine Jesus showing as He healed the broken.

There was something sacred in the way he leaned over his son—carefully, patiently, gently. Each touch seemed to say, "I forgive you. I love you. You are still my son." It reminded me of how God tends to our own wounds those seen and unseen, when we've made mistakes and gone astray.

In that small bedroom, love became holy. Jay wasn't just caring for our son's injuries; he was ministering to his spirit. It was as though he were tending to the wounds of Christ Himself, as Jesus endured the stripes that would one day bring us all healing.

That day, I saw what **Psalm 103:13** truly means *"As a father has compassion on his children, so the Lord has compassion on those who fear Him."* Compassion isn't just a feeling it's an act of grace, freely given even when pain is still fresh. Through Jay's hands, I saw God's hands. Through his care, I saw redemption. And through it all, I was reminded that love true love heals more than just the body; it restores the soul.

May they come to know You personally as their loving Father and Savior. We ask for Your divine presence to surround them each day, bringing comfort, strength, and reassurance. Let Your peace, which surpasses all understanding, guard their hearts and minds in Christ Jesus. May they experience a deep sense of security and belonging in Your love. Lord, we pray for their emotional healing and spiritual growth. Help us to nurture their faith and trust in You, fostering an environment where they can flourish and thrive. Give us patience and wisdom to care for them with grace and compassion, showing them Your unconditional love through our words and actions. May our home be a sanctuary of peace and joy, where Your presence is felt and Your name is praised. Use us, Lord, as instruments of Your peace, guiding these children towards a future filled with hope and promise. We commit their lives into Your hands, trusting in Your faithfulness and goodness. Thank You for the privilege of witnessing Your transformative work in their lives.

In Jesus' Name I Pray, Amen.

Day Twenty-Four ~ Taught by the Lord

Scripture:

> *"All your children will be taught by the Lord, and great will be their peace."*
> *Isaiah 54:13*

Prayer

Heavenly Father,

We come before You with hearts full of gratitude for the privilege of serving as foster and adoptive parents to the precious children You have entrusted to our care. Your Word in *Isaiah 54:13* declares, *"All your children shall be taught by the Lord, and great shall be the peace of your children."*

Lord, thank You for this promise a reminder that You, above all, are the ultimate Teacher and Guide in our children's lives. We ask that You pour out Your wisdom and understanding upon them. Reveal Your truth to their hearts and help them to know You personally as their loving Father and Savior.

May Your divine presence surround them each day, bringing comfort, strength, and assurance. Let Your peace which surpasses all understanding guard their hearts and minds in Christ Jesus. May they experience the deep security that comes from knowing they are loved, chosen, and never alone.

Father, we pray for their emotional healing and spiritual growth. Help us to nurture their faith and trust in You, creating a home where they can flourish in safety, love, and joy. Grant us patience and grace to model Your character gentle, compassionate, and steadfast so that through our lives, they may see Yours.

May our home be a sanctuary of peace and praise, where Your presence is felt and Your name is honored. Use us, Lord, as instruments of Your peace, guiding these children toward the bright future You have prepared for them a future filled with hope, promise, and purpose.

We commit their lives into Your hands, trusting in Your faithfulness and goodness. Thank You for the privilege of witnessing Your transforming work in their hearts and lives.

In Jesus' Name I pray, Amen.

Reflection: A Father and a Son, in God's Presence

The day Mekhi rededicated his life to God was quiet and unplanned just him and his father at the church. There was no crowd, no music, no ceremony. Mekhi had been at the church helping out, doing what he often did serving, working, and giving his time. It was in that familiar space of service that the Lord met him in a deeply personal way.

When Jay arrived at the church that day, he hadn't expected anything out of the ordinary. But as he walked in and saw Mekhi, something in the atmosphere felt different peaceful, yet powerful. Mekhi's heart had already been stirred. As they stood together in that still, sacred space, he began to pray not with practiced words, but from a heart ready to come home to God.

There were no rehearsed speeches or emotional displays just sincerity, repentance, and the unmistakable presence of the Holy Spirit. Jay stood beside Mekhi, his hand resting gently on Mekhi's shoulder as tears filled both their eyes. It was a special moment a father witnessing his son's heart turn fully back to the Lord.

When Mekhi lifted his head, there was a new calm in his expression a peace that words could not describe. The same hands that had once held wounds were now lifted in surrender. It was as though heaven itself leaned down to affirm that promise in *Isaiah 54:1*

"All your children will be taught by the Lord, and great will be their peace."

That day wasn't planned by man but orchestrated by God. It was a reminder that our children don't have to be perfect for God to call them; they just have to be present when He speaks. In the quietness of the sanctuary, with no one else around, a father watched his son's spirit restored, and through it, saw the compassion and faithfulness of the Heavenly Father reflected right before his eyes.

Reflection of the Day:

_____

_____

_____

_____

_____

_____

_____

_____

_____

_____

_____

_____

_____

Day Twenty-Five ~ A Heritage from the Lord

Scripture

> *"Behold, children are a heritage from the Lord, the fruit of the womb is a reward."*
> *Psalm 127:3*

Prayer

Heavenly Father,

We come before You with grateful hearts, acknowledging the precious gift of children You have entrusted to our care. Your Word reminds us that they are a heritage from You, a blessing beyond measure and a reflection of Your unfailing love and grace.

Lord, we thank You for the joy and wonder our children bring into our lives. Each smile, each laugh, and even each challenge is a reminder of the sacred responsibility You have given us. We celebrate them as the fruit of Your goodness, the living rewards of Your promise, and the evidence of Your divine favor upon our families.

Grant us wisdom and patience as we nurture and guide them in Your ways. Help us to teach with love, correct with gentleness, and lead by example so they may grow to know You personally and follow Your path with confidence and faith.

Strengthen us as parents to remain steadfast and compassionate, trusting You in every season of their growth. Instill in our children a deep awareness of Your presence and purpose for their lives. May they become lights in this world rooted in faith, walking in grace, and reflecting Your glory in all they do.

Lord, continue to bless our families with unity, peace, and understanding. May our homes be filled with laughter, learning, and love that honors You. We thank You for the heritage You've given us and for the privilege of shaping hearts that belong to You.

In Jesus' Name I pray, Amen.

Reflection: A Promise in His Hands

I remember when Jay Timothy Harrison Jr. was born on September 13, 1988, in Chester, Pennsylvania. The pregnancy had been normal, but after almost thirty hours of labor, the doctors decided to deliver him by C-section. My husband, who was working in the nursing field at the time, was allowed to remain with me through the entire process.

At exactly 6:12 p.m., our son made his debut into the world. Exhausted but relieved, I waited to hold him, and then I heard laughter ripple through the delivery room slowly as I began to wake up from the surgery. The nurses, the doctor, and even my husband began exclaiming in amazement. "Look at that! He came out with his fist clenched, but with his thumb up!"

I didn't see it right away, but when they brought him to me, I understood why everyone was talking. His tiny hand was still balled into a fist, that perfect little thumb pointing upward as if heaven itself had placed a seal of approval over his arrival. In that moment, I knew this was the beginning of something great for the Harrison family.

Jay Jr.'s entry into the world reminded me that every child is born with purpose, unique, chosen, and divinely appointed. His first gesture, that little thumbs-up, felt like God whispering, "It's all going to be okay."

Psalm 127:3 says, "Behold, children are a heritage from the Lord, the fruit of the womb is a reward." And that day, holding my son for the first time, I understood that verse in a brand-new way. Jay wasn't just our baby, he was God's promise in human form, entrusted to us as part of a greater story that was still unfolding.

Reflection of the Day

_____

_____

_____

_____

_____

_____

_____

_____

_____

_____

_____

_____

_____

Day Twenty-Six ~ Loved Into Family

Scripture

> **"Children's children are the crown of old men, and the glory of children is their father."** *Proverbs 17:6*

Prayer

Heavenly Father,

Our hearts are filled with gratitude and awe of You, recognizing the profound truth that children's children are the crown of old men and that children are the glory of their father.

We thank You for the generations that come before and after us for the joy, pride, and purpose found in our children and our children's children. They are living testaments of Your faithfulness and the beauty of Your divine design for family.

Lord, we ask for Your continued guidance and blessing upon our families. Help us to honor the legacy of faith and love You have placed before us. Grant us grace to nurture with wisdom, to lead with humility, and to love with the same compassion You show to us.

Teach us to cherish the laughter, growth, and even the challenges that come with parenting and grandparenting. Let our lives be examples of steadfast faith reminders to those who come after us that Your love endures through every generation.

May our homes overflow with peace, unity, and joy. Let every moment spent with our children and grandchildren reflect Your goodness, and may the legacy we leave be one of faith, love, and unwavering trust in You.

In Jesus' Name I pray, Amen.

Reflection: I'm Adopted

At the beginning of the school year at Widener Elementary, Micah's class was given an assignment to write about their families. Excitedly, Micah wrote about the people he loved most his mom, dad, brothers, and sisters. He proudly described his big brother Jay T, who play-boxed with him, and his sister, Romesha, whom he once rescued during a game of hide and seek that went terribly wrong. Romesha had chosen to hide in the dryer, and Micah had been the hero who found her just in time.

He also wrote about Chewey, the big, lovable family dog he could climb on, though he admitted Harpo barked far too much for his liking. Micah shared how much he loved family trips, game nights with Uno, and going to church together. His paper painted a beautiful picture of joy, belonging, and love.

But there was one part of his story he didn't include he didn't mention being adopted. It wasn't because he was ashamed; he simply didn't yet know how to explain it.

A few weeks later, Micah came home visibly upset. His teacher had accidentally mentioned to the class that he was adopted, and some of the students began teasing him. They made hurtful comments like, "Your family found you!" They laughed in ways that made Micah's heart ache. The teasing grew heavier each day until he started to dread going to school.

One evening, unable to hold it in any longer, Micah told his father what had been happening. Jay listened carefully, his face filled with concern and compassion. After a moment of silence, he spoke gently:

"Micah," he said, "no matter what anyone says, we love you with all our hearts. You are part of this family, and nothing can ever change that. You are loved by us, and you are loved by God. There's a verse in the Bible *Psalm 68:6* that says, *'God sets the lonely in families.'* You were always meant to be part of our family, and we will always be here for you."

Those words settled deeply in Micah's heart. Though the teasing didn't stop overnight, something inside him shifted. He began to walk with quiet confidence, no longer defined by what others said, but by the love that surrounded him at home. He understood now that adoption wasn't something to hide it was a beautiful reflection of God's love and purpose for his life.

Micah realized that his story was one of grace that just as God brings us into His family through love, he too had been loved into family. And in that truth, he found peace.

Reflection of the Day:

_____

_____

_____

_____

_____

_____

_____

_____

_____

_____

_____

_____

_____

_____

Day Twenty-Seven ~ The Heart of a Child

Scripture:

> *"At that time the disciples came to Jesus, saying, 'Who then is greatest in the kingdom of heaven?' Then Jesus called a little child to Him, set him in the midst of them, and said, 'Assuredly, I say to you, unless you are converted and become as little children, you will by no means enter the kingdom of heaven." Matthew 18:1–3*

Prayer:

Heavenly Father,

We enter into Your presence with humble hearts, reflecting on the words of Your Son, Jesus, who reminded us that the way to Your Kingdom is found through the heart of a child.

Lord, teach us to walk in that same spirit of purity, humility, and trust. Help us to embrace a childlike faith one that believes without doubting, hopes without hesitation, and loves without condition. Strip away our pride, fear, and self-reliance so that we may approach You with open hands and open hearts, fully dependent on Your grace.

Grant us the courage to let go of our own plans and ambitions, seeking instead to follow Your will with the same eagerness and surrender that children have when they trust those who love them. Remind us that true greatness in Your Kingdom isn't found in status or strength, but in humility, compassion, and simple faith.

Help us to see others through the lens of innocence and love, offering grace where the world would offer judgment, and patience where the world would give up. May our lives reflect the joy, honesty, and wonder that come from walking closely with You.

As we learn to become more like little children curious, trusting, and full of awe—draw us nearer to Your heart. Let our faith inspire others to do the same, that together we may live as reflections of Your Kingdom here on earth.

In Jesus' Name I pray, Amen.

Reflection: A Father's Lesson on God's Heart

I remember one evening when Jay sat down with the boys to talk about God. Micah and Mekhi had been full of questions that night deep, thoughtful ones that only children could ask with such honesty.

"Does God actually hear our prayers?" one of them asked. "And does He get mad at us when we don't listen?"

Their questions were simple, yet profound, echoing the same curiosity that Jesus spoke of when He told the disciples to become as little children.

As usual, my husband the great orator that he is began to explain with clarity, love, and patience. He didn't rush or offer a textbook answer. Instead, he spoke gently, painting a picture of God's heart that even the youngest mind could understand.

He told them that yes, God hears every prayer every whisper, every sigh, every tear. He explained that God's love doesn't fade when we make mistakes or fail to listen; instead, His heart remains open, always ready to forgive and draw us back close to Him.

"The thing about God," Jay said, "is that He's not looking for perfection. He's looking for honesty. He wants your heart more than your words. When you talk to Him, He listens not because you're perfect, but because you're His."

The boys sat quietly for a moment, absorbing every word. I could see their little faces soften with understanding and peace. There was something sacred about that conversation a father revealing the tenderness of the Heavenly Father to his sons.

That night reminded me of *Matthew 18:3,* where Jesus said that unless we become as little children, we cannot enter the Kingdom of Heaven. Watching Jay speak to the boys, I understood that truth in a deeper way. Childlike faith isn't about knowing all the answers it's about asking the right questions with a heart willing to trust.

In that quiet family moment, faith was passed down not through a Sunday morning sermon, but through love.

Reflection of the Day

_____

_____

_____

_____

_____

_____

_____

_____

_____

_____

_____

_____

_____

Day Twenty-Eight ~ God Already Knew You

Scripture:

> *"Before I formed you in the womb I knew you; before you were born I sanctified you; I ordained you a prophet to the nations." Jeremiah 1:5*

Prayer:

Heavenly Father,
We come before You reflecting on Your profound words in *Jeremiah 1:5*, which remind us that You knew us before we were even formed in the womb and that You set us apart for Your divine purpose.

Lord, we are humbled by the knowledge that our lives are not random but are intricately woven into Your perfect plan. Thank You for the purpose You have assigned to each of us and for the care with which You have shaped our lives.

Help us to embrace our identity as Your beloved creations chosen, known, and deeply loved. Grant us wisdom to discern Your will and courage to walk in the paths You have prepared for us. May we always remember that our worth is defined not by our past or our circumstances, but by Your eternal love and calling.

Equip us with strength to fulfill the assignments You've entrusted to us. In moments of uncertainty, remind us that You have already gone before us. Let Your presence steady our hearts and renew our confidence as we walk in step with Your purpose.

Thank You, Lord, for the assurance that we are known, loved, and appointed for greatness according to Your divine plan.

In Jesus' Name I pray, Amen.

Reflection: God Already Knew You

God led us into fostering after we had already opened our home and hearts to more than fourteen children. Fostering wasn't something Jay and I had initially planned for it was something God gently placed in our path. As we cared for child after child, each with their own story and need for love, we began to see how intentional His hand truly was.

Then one day, our lives were changed forever. Two energetic, bright-eyed boys named Micah and Mekhi came through our door. With their laughter, curiosity, and boundless energy, they brought light into our lives in ways we could have never anticipated both through the joys and the challenges.

The first few years of their lives had been filled with uncertainty, and hardship circumstances no child should ever have to endure. But from the moment they entered our home, it was clear that God's hand was upon them. Their past did not define them. Their resilience, their laughter, and their capacity to love spoke of something greater, a divine favor that was already shaping their future.

Through fostering and ultimately adopting Mekhi, and Micah we witnessed firsthand the truth of *Jeremiah 1:5*. God's love and purpose for a life are not determined by how that life begins, but by His eternal plan. What started as an act of obedience to opening our home to children in need became a testimony of His faithfulness. The process was not always easy, but God's presence was undeniable every step of the way.

We watched them grow strong, compassionate, and full of joy. Their hearts overflowed with kindness, and their laughter filled every corner of our home. Despite what they had endured, God's redemption was evident in their lives. He had written a new story one of healing, belonging, and hope.

Mekhi, and Micah are living proof that God's favor cannot be limited by the past. His love transcends every barrier, every label, and every wound. Long before we ever knew them, God did. He knew their laughter would fill our home. He knew their hearts would expand ours. And He knew that their story would be a reflection of His one of love that restores, redeems, and never lets go.

Reflection of the Day

_____

_____

_____

_____

_____

_____

_____

_____

_____

_____

_____

_____

_____

_____

Day Twenty-Nine ~ Wonderfully Made by God

Scripture:

> *"For You formed my inward parts;*
> *You covered me in my mother's womb.*
> *I will praise You, for I am fearfully and*
> *wonderfully made;*
> *Marvelous are Your works, and that my*
> *soul knows very well." Psalm 139:13–14*

Prayer
Heavenly Father,
We come before You in awe, reflecting on the beautiful truth found in Psalm 139:13–14. You formed us with intention and love, shaping every detail of our being before we ever took our first breath. You knew us completely our strengths, our weaknesses, and the purpose You placed within each of us.

Lord, thank You for the care and precision with which You created us. Every part of who we are bears the imprint of Your divine design. Help us to embrace this truth fully, to see ourselves not through the lens of comparison or insecurity, but through the lens of Your perfect love.

When we struggle with doubt or feel unworthy, You remind us that we are fearfully and wonderfully made crafted by the Creator of the universe, designed with beauty, value, and purpose. Let this knowledge fill our hearts with gratitude and confidence, knowing that we are Your masterpiece.

Teach us to walk in the purpose for which we were created. May we use our gifts to serve others, honor You with our lives, and reflect Your glory in all that we do. And when we are tempted to forget our worth, draw us back to this truth, that we are loved, chosen, and made marvelous by Your hands.

In Jesus' Holy Name we pray, Amen.

Reflection: More Than a Mark

I'll never forget the day Micah came home with a new tattoo right above his left eyebrow. It read, "Prolific." My first reaction came out before I could even filter it: "Boy, you out here marking up your face?"

I was irritated, and maybe even a little heartbroken. I couldn't understand why he would choose something so permanent, something that the world would see before they ever got the chance to know him.

But after my calm-down period, I did what mothers often have to do instead of talking, I listened. Micah talked about why he did it, about what the word meant to him, about wanting to leave his mark on the world and live up to something greater. Beneath his words, I could hear what he was really saying: "I need to know who I am. I need to know that my life means something."

In that moment, God reminded me that our children's choices especially the ones we don't always understand often come from a place of searching. Micah wasn't rebelling; he was reaching for identity, for affirmation, for belonging.

Once I set my irritation aside, I told him, "That tattoo doesn't define who you are. Your character does. Your purpose comes from who God says you are not from anything written on your skin." I reminded him that he was wonderfully made, designed with purpose long before he ever thought about a tattoo.

I'm still not particularly thrilled about that tattoo, but I've come to see it differently. It's part of his journey his story of learning, of becoming, of discovering his identity in Christ.

Psalm 139 reminds us that we are fearfully and wonderfully made crafted by God with intention and love. And as I looked at my son, I realized that even with the ink on his face, he was still God's masterpiece unique, chosen, and marked by grace.

Reflection of the Day

_____

_____

_____

_____

_____

_____

_____

_____

_____

_____

_____

_____

_____

_____

Day Thirty ~ Honoring the Promise

Scripture

> *"Children, obey your parents in the Lord,*
> *for this is right.*
> *'Honor your father and mother,' which is*
> *the first commandment with promise:*
> *'that it may be well with you and you may*
> *live long on the earth." Ephesians 6:1–3*

Prayer:

Heavenly Father,

We come before You with hearts full of gratitude, reflecting on the truth of *Ephesians 6:1–3*, where You call us to honor and obey our parents a commandment wrapped in Your promise of blessing and long life.

Lord, thank You for the gift of family and for the parents, guardians, and mentors who have guided us along the way. Help us to honor them with respect, love, and a grateful heart, recognizing the important role they play as vessels of Your wisdom and care. May our obedience be rooted not in obligation, but in love and reverence for You.

For parents, we ask for Your grace and patience. Strengthen us to lead with compassion and understanding, to correct with gentleness, and to nurture our children with the same love You so freely give to us. Help us to live as examples of faith, humility, and honor modeling the values we hope to see reflected in our children.

Lord, let our homes be places where love is practiced, forgiveness is extended, and respect flows freely between generations. May our relationships within the family reflect the unity and grace found in You.

We thank You for the blessings that flow from obedience and for the promise that honoring our parents brings peace and prosperity. Help us to live in a way that brings glory to Your name and preserves the legacy of faith and love for generations to come.

In Jesus' Name I pray, Amen.

Final Reflection ~ A Legacy of Unshakable Faith

As this 30-day journey of prayer comes to a close, I am
reminded that the true legacy we leave behind is not
found in possessions or accomplishments, but in faith
the kind of faith that endures through seasons of joy,
loss, and redemption.

Through every moment from laughter-filled family
nights to hospital waiting rooms, from quiet prayers
whispered in the dark to testimonies shared in the light
God has proven Himself faithful. Each page of this
journey reflects His unwavering hand, guiding, healing,
and restoring.

The story of our family has never been one of
perfection, but one of promise. It is the story of a God
who never lets go, who redeems broken places, and who
calls each of us by name before we ever take our first
breath. It's the story of learning to trust even when we
don't understand, of remaining steadfast and unmovable
when the winds of life blow hard, and of standing firm
on the foundation of faith that cannot be shaken.

Our children Jay Timothy Jr., Juanita, Jessika, Robert,
Romesha Katyce, and Brittany each carry a piece of this
legacy. Their lives are living proof that God's promises
never fail. Through their laughter, their growth, their

challenges, and their triumphs, we have seen the evidence of His love at work. They are the fruit of prayers prayed in faith, and tears sown in hope. They are our heritage, and they are God's reward.

And though the road has not been without pain, we have learned that steadfast faith doesn't mean life will be easy, it simply means God will always be present. It means trusting Him when the outcome is unclear, praising Him when the heart is heavy, and holding on to Him when everything else seems uncertain.

Our legacy, then, is simple to trust God fully, to love deeply, and to walk boldly in faith that will not be moved. We have seen His goodness in every season, and we stand as witnesses that His Word is true:

> *"Therefore, my beloved brethren, be ye steadfast, unmovable, always abounding in the work of the Lord, forasmuch as ye know that your labour is not in vain in the Lord." 1 Corinthians 15:58*

This is the legacy we leave not just in words, but in faith lived out daily.
A legacy that says: we trusted God… and He never failed us.

Reflection of the Day

_____

_____

_____

_____

_____

_____

_____

_____

_____

_____

_____

_____

_____

_____

_____

_____

Bonus Day ~ The Healing Power of Words

Scripture

> *"The words of the reckless pierce like swords, but the tongue of the wise brings healing." Proverbs 12:18*

Prayer:
Father,
We come before You with humble hearts, recognizing the power and weight our words carry—especially in the lives of the children You've entrusted to our care. Your Word reminds us that reckless speech can wound deeply, but that wise and loving words have the power to bring healing, restoration, and hope.

Lord, grant us the wisdom to speak life. Let every word that leaves our lips be guided by Your Spirit—filled with kindness, patience, and grace. Help us to be mindful of how our voices shape the hearts of those who listen, especially the tender spirits of the children who look to us for love and affirmation.

Teach us to nurture their gifts through encouragement and to strengthen their confidence through compassion. May our words uplift and inspire, reminding them that they are valuable, capable, and wonderfully made in Your image.

Surround our children with wise and faithful influences—people who will speak truth and love into their lives. Let our homes and classrooms be sanctuaries of peace where words heal rather than harm, where correction comes with gentleness, and where love is expressed through listening and understanding.

Lord, continue to guide us as we raise, teach, and support these precious gifts of Yours. May our example and our words reflect Your heart, drawing them closer to You and to the purpose You have prepared for their lives.

We thank You for entrusting us with such sacred responsibility, and we ask that every word we speak brings healing, strength, and joy to those we love.

In Jesus' Name, Amen.

Reflection: Healing Through an Apology

There was a time when I had to apologize to Mekhi. It started one afternoon when I discovered that someone had written all over the wall in the hallway. Without much thought, I assumed Mekhi had done it. Micah, his twin, confirmed my suspicion, and I reacted in frustration—disappointed that he would do something like that.

Later that evening, after things had calmed down, I learned the truth. Through what the kids call a little "ear hustling," I overheard Micah confess that he was the one who had written on the wall. He admitted he had blamed his brother to get back at him for telling on him about something that had happened at school. My heart sank.

I immediately went to find Mekhi. I told him the truth—that I had made a mistake. I explained that I should have come to him first, spoken with him, and given him the chance to explain before assuming the worst. I looked him in the eye and said, "I'm sorry."

What happened next reminded me of the very heart of Proverbs 12:18—that our words can wound, but they can also heal. Mekhi didn't hesitate. He smiled softly and said, "It's okay, Mom."

In that moment, forgiveness and understanding filled the space where hurt had been. My apology became a bridge that restored trust. It was a gentle reminder that even as parents, we don't always get it right—but when we humble ourselves and speak truth in love, healing follows.

That day, I realized how much our words matter. A harsh word can tear down, but a sincere apology can rebuild. Through that small but powerful moment, I saw God's grace at work—not just in me, but in my son's ability to forgive so freely.

The tongue of the wise truly does bring healing, and sometimes, wisdom begins with the courage to say, "I was wrong."

Reflection of the Day

_____

_____

_____

_____

_____

_____

_____

_____

_____

_____

_____

_____

The Birth of LaJaTimIse

LaJaTimIse was formed out of **love and a little bit of boredom.**

In 2011, our nephew Jeremiah would visit us during the summer. From a very young age, he showed a strong interest in the drums — and so did Mekhi. The two could never agree on who would play, so naturally, we ended up with *two drummers!* I would sing, and everyone else would join in with laughter, rhythm, and joy.

Micah was always nearby with a tambourine or maracas, and sometimes he'd jump in on the drums too. What started as a simple family pastime quickly turned into something much more — a beautiful expression of togetherness, music, and love.

Mom would often come in and record us during our "rehearsals," capturing those moments of spontaneous harmony and joy that filled our home.

The name **LaJaTimIse** was born from the combination of our middle names
— **La** for *Lavonne*, **Ja** for *James*, **Tim** for *Timothy*, and **Ise** for *Denise*. Every capital letter carries a piece of our story, our bond, and our shared laughter.

Scripture:
"Make a joyful noise unto the Lord, all ye lands. Serve the Lord with gladness: come before his presence with singing."
— Psalm 100:1–2 (KJV)

-Romesha Harrison

Author's Note ~ A Legacy of Love and Faith

As this devotional journey draws to a close, my heart overflows with gratitude for the lessons learned, the prayers whispered, and the love that continues to bind our family together. Thirty Days of Prayer for Foster Parents & Adoptive Families: The Twinz Legacy Edition is more than a collection of prayers and reflections it is a testimony of God's faithfulness, grace, and the unbreakable bond of family.

Each story, each prayer, and each scripture reflects the heart of a mother, a wife, and a believer who has seen God move in both mountain-top moments and valleys of pain. Through it all, I've learned that faith is not about understanding every step, but trusting that every step is guided by the One who knows the way.

This devotional is dedicated in loving memory of Mekhi James Harrison and Micah Timothy Harrison; "The Twinz," whose lives continue to inspire faith, strength, laughter, and love. Their legacy reminds us that even in life's hardest moments, God's presence remains constant, and His purpose still unfolds in beauty and grace.

To every parent, foster parent, adoptive family, and caregiver may this devotional be a reminder that your labor of love is not in vain. You are shaping hearts, planting seeds, and building legacies that will echo for generations.

> *"Therefore, my beloved brethren, be ye steadfast, unmovable, always abounding in the work of the Lord, forasmuch as ye know that your labour is not in vain in the Lord."*
> *1 Corinthians 15:58*

With all my heart, I thank you for joining me on this journey of prayer, reflection, and faith.

All proceeds from this devotional will go to The Twinz Foundation, established in loving memory of Mekhi and Micah Harrison. Through this foundation, their light continues to shine bringing hope, encouragement, and support to families and children in need.

May the legacy of love, faith, and steadfast trust in God continue through every life touched by this work.

With love and gratitude,
Crystal Denise Harrison, M.Ed.
Author & Founder, The Twinz Foundation

Daily Prayer Request Log

Date Request Made	Prayer Request	Date Prayer Request Answered

Date Request Made	Prayer Request	Date Prayer Request Answered

Date Request Made	Prayer Request	Date Prayer Request Answered

Harrison Family Purpose Statement

Our purpose as the (insert your family's last name) is to build a loving, supportive, and purposeful life together, grounded in our values and committed to our shared goals.

1. **Love and Connection:** We strive to create a home where love and respect are the foundation of our relationships. Our goal is to support and uplift each other, fostering deep connections and a sense of belonging.
2. **Faith and Integrity:** We are dedicated to living out our faith and values with honesty and integrity. Our actions and decisions are guided by principles of compassion, justice, and respect for all.
3. **Growth and Learning:** We are committed to personal and collective growth. We encourage each family member to pursue their passions and interests, support lifelong learning, and embrace opportunities for self-improvement.
4. **Service and Impact:** We aim to make a positive impact in our community and the world. Through acts of service and kindness, we seek to contribute to the well-being of others and promote a spirit of generosity and compassion.

5. **Joy and Celebration:** We cherish the moments we share and celebrate our achievements and milestones with joy and gratitude. We believe in finding happiness in our everyday lives and making the most of our time together.

6. **Legacy and Values:** We are committed to leaving a legacy of love, faith, and respect for future generations. Our purpose is to instill these values in our children and to build a strong family legacy that reflects our core beliefs and aspirations.

Together, we embrace this "Purpose Statement" with dedication and enthusiasm, working as a family to achieve our goals and live out our values every day.

Our Family Mission Statement

We are the Harrison Family, united by our love for one another and guided by our faith and values.

1. **Love and Respect:** We commit to loving and respecting each member of our family, showing kindness, patience, and understanding in all our interactions.
2. **Faith and Growth:** We will nurture our spiritual growth by seeking God's guidance, fostering a strong faith, and supporting each other in our spiritual journeys.
3. **Honesty and Integrity:** We pledge to live with honesty and integrity, being truthful and trustworthy in all our dealings, and holding each other accountable with grace.
4. **Support and Encouragement:** We will support and encourage each other in our individual dreams and aspirations, celebrating each achievement and offering comfort and strength in times of challenge.
5. **Learning and Growth:** We are dedicated to lifelong learning and personal development, seeking knowledge and wisdom, and growing together as a family through shared experiences and education.

6. **Service and Compassion:** We aim to serve others with compassion and generosity, reaching out to those in need and making a positive impact in our community and beyond.
7. **Joy and Gratitude:** We will embrace each day with joy and gratitude, cherishing the moments we share and appreciating the blessings of our family life.

Together, we strive to live these values daily, building a home of love, faith in God, and unity where each member feels valued, supported, and empowered.

Our Family Vision Statement

As the Harrison Family, our vision is to create a loving, supportive, and vibrant home where each member thrives and our shared values guide us toward a fulfilling and impactful life.

1. Unified in Purpose: We envision a family united by a common purpose, where each individual feels connected and valued, and we work together to achieve our collective goals and dreams.
2. Spiritual Fulfillment: We seek to deepen our spiritual lives, fostering a strong relationship with God and living out our faith through our actions, relationships, and service to others.
3. Health and Well-being: We aspire to cultivate a lifestyle that promotes physical, emotional, and mental well-being, supporting each other in living healthy, balanced lives.
4. Continuous Growth: We are committed to lifelong learning and personal development, encouraging curiosity, resilience, and adaptability as we navigate life's challenges and opportunities.
5. Compassionate Service: We strive to make a positive difference in the world by serving others

with compassion and generosity, contributing to our community and beyond with humility and kindness.

6. **Joyful Living:** We aim to create a home filled with laughter, joy, and gratitude, cherishing each moment together and celebrating our achievements and milestones.

7. **Legacy of Love:** We envision leaving a legacy of love, integrity, and respect that will inspire future generations, fostering strong family bonds and upholding the values that have guided us.

Together, we are dedicated to living out this vision, building a future where our family's love and commitment shine brightly, guiding us toward a life of purpose, fulfillment, and lasting impact.

Daily Focus Scriptures for Faith

1. Philippians 4:13

2. Proverbs 3:5-6

3. Ephesians 6:10

4. Jeremiah 29:11

5. Matthew 6:33

6. Isaiah 41:10

7. Hebrews 11:1

8. 2 Corinthians 5:7

9. 1 Corinthians 16:13

10. Lamentations 3:24

11. Joshua 1:9

12. Hebrews 10:23

13. Psalm 71:14

14. Psalm 146:5

15. Proverbs 10:28

16. 2 Corinthians 9:8

17. Nehemiah 8:10

18. 2 Timothy 1:7

19. Isaiah 40:31

20. Psalm 18:32

21. Jeremiah 17:7

22. Psalm 112:7

23. Nahum 1:7

24. Psalm 1:1-3

25. Deuteronomy 31:6

26. 2 Samuel 22:33

27. Psalm 20:7

28. Isaiah 12:2

29. Psalm 56:3

30. Romans 12:12

Family Resources

1. **National Foster Care Coalition**

   - Website: nfcc.us

2. **Child Welfare Information Gateway**

   - Website: childwelfare.gov

3. **AdoptUSKids**

   - Website: adoptuskids.org

4. **The Dave Thomas Foundation for Adoption**

   - Website:

     davethomasfoundation.org

Local Support

5. **Foster Care Agencies**

   - Look for local agencies that offer support groups, training, and resources for foster families.

6. **Adoption Agencies/Foster Care Agencies -**

Many agencies provide counseling, training, and
resources for adoptive families.

- New Foundations Inc.

- Children's Choice

- Open Arms Adoption Network

- Adoptions From the Heart

Online Communities

7. **Social Media Groups**

- Search for groups focused on
foster care and adoption for peer
support and shared resources.

Educational Resources

8. The National Child Traumatic Stress Network (NCTSN)

- Website: nctsn.org
- Offers resources on trauma-informed care for children in foster and adoptive placements.

9. Attachment and Trauma Network

- Website: attachmenttraumanetwork.org
- Provides information on attachment issues and trauma-informed parenting.

Legal Resources

11. American Bar Association (ABA)

- Website: americanbar.org- Offers resources related to adoption law and foster care.

12. National Adoption Center

- Website: adopt.org-Provides legal and practical guidance on the adoption process.

Financial Resources

13. Adoption Tax Credit

- Information on the federal adoption tax credit can be found on the IRS website: irs.gov.

14. Grants and Scholarships

- Organizations like the **Dave Thomas Foundation** and local

community foundations often
provide financial assistance for
adoption.

- The Twinz Foundation

Mental Health Resources

15. Therapy and Counseling

- Look for therapists specializing in
trauma, attachment, and parenting
in foster/adoptive situations.

Books and Publications

- "The Connected Child" by Karyn Purvis, David
Cross, and Wendy Sunshine

- "Adoption: Choosing It, Living It, Loving It" by
Laura K. Dyer

- "Adopted for Life" by Russell D. Moore
- "Adoption: The Heart of the Matter" by Steven Curtis Chapman
- "The Adoption Life Cycle" by Elizabeth Bartholet
- "Being Adopted: The Lifelong Journey" by David S. Kessler
- "In On It: What Adoptive Parents Would Like You to Know About Adoption" by Julia Feininger
- "The Gospel and Adoption" by Jedd Medefind
- "Orphanology" by Tony Merida and Rick Morton
- "The Connected Child" by Karyn Purvis, David Cross, and Wendy Sunshine

- "The Spirit of Adoption" by John and Helen D. Smith
- "Every Good and Perfect Gift" by Jerry and Marilyn W. Krieger
- "Twenty Things Adopted Kids Wish Their Adoptive Parents Knew" by Sherrie Eldridge
- "The Spirit of Adoption" by John and Helen D. Smith
- "Adoption Parenting: Creating a Toolbox, Building Connections" by Jean MacLeod and Sheena Macrae

Conferences and Workshops

17. Local and National Conferences

- Attend workshops and conferences focused on adoption and foster care to connect with other families and professionals.

To: Jeremiah Lavan Harrison

I want to take a moment to express my heartfelt gratitude for the way you've continued to uphold the values and standards your mother has instilled in you especially in a time when so many young people have chosen to compromise under the weight of peer pressure. Your steadfast commitment to integrity, excellence, and strong moral character is truly inspiring to witness.

In a world where many compromise their ideals, standards, and morals for the sake of attention, fun, or fleeting popularity, your resolve to remain true to who you are stands as a beacon of hope. You remind us that integrity, discipline, and faith still matter, and that they can shine as powerful examples to others, especially to the youth watching your life.

Thank you for being a shining example of what it means to walk upright and with purpose. Please know that your strength, determination, and quiet leadership have not gone unnoticed. You embody the kind of faith and resilience that changes lives, and causes legacy.

In the words of **Micah Timothy Harrison**, *"Bro, you gotta keep running the race if you want to win!"*

You were a voice of reason in *The Twinz'* lives, and your Pop-Pop and I are deeply grateful that you chose to be an example when many both young and old had the opportunity to do so, but didn't. You were more than a nephew; you became a brother the third of the "triplets," as Mekhi used to say with pride.

We are so proud of you, Jeremiah. Continue to walk with purpose, lead with faith, and let your light shine wherever life takes you.

Wishing you continued strength, grace, and success in all that you do.

With all our love,
 Pop-Pop & Nana

The Twinz Foundation

Mission Statement

"Let your light so shine before men, that they may see your good works and glorify your Father which is in heaven." Matthew 5:16 (KJV)

The Twinz Foundation is dedicated to empowering students and their families by providing essential financial support for educational, social, medical, and extracurricular needs.

Our mission is to ensure that every student from elementary through high school has access to the vital resources necessary for success. These include book bags, school uniforms, supplies, back-to-school essentials, sports physicals, high school graduation photos and rings, and college entrance exam fees.

In addition to meeting academic needs, The Twinz Foundation also supports families by funding field trips and other enriching experiences that many must often forgo due to financial hardship.

By removing financial barriers, we aim to open doors of opportunity helping students reach their full potential academically, socially, and personally. Through this commitment, The Twinz Foundation seeks to create a lasting impact, fostering confidence, achievement, and hope for every child and family we serve.

Twinz Foundation Vision Statement

*"For I know the plans I have for you," declares the
Lord, "plans to prosper you and not to harm you, plans
to give you hope and a future."
Jeremiah 29:11 (KJV)*

At **The Twinz Foundation**, our vision is to create a
future where every student has equal access to the
resources and opportunities needed to thrive
academically, spiritually, emotionally, physically, and
personally.

We envision a world where financial barriers no longer
hinder a student's educational journey; where every
child can embrace learning, growth, and discovery
without limitation; and where every family can support
their child's dreams with confidence and dignity.

Through our unwavering commitment to educational
equity, spiritual growth, and community support, we
strive to inspire and empower the next generation to
reach their fullest potential. Our goal is to equip each
student with the opportunities, tools, resources, and
encouragement needed to pursue their purpose and
fulfill their God-given destiny without limitations.

Together, we believe in building not just scholars, but strong, faith-filled leaders who will impact their communities and carry forward a legacy of excellence, compassion, and hope.

Thank you mikey621- You and your wife are phenomenal!